The Mathematics of Turfgrass Maintenance

Second Edition

Nick E. Christians, Ph.D.
Iowa State University
Department of Horticulture
Ames, Iowa

Michael L. Agnew, Ph.D.
Novartis Corporation
Crop Protection Division
Turf and Ornaments Department
Greensboro, North Carolina

Ann Arbor Press, Inc.
Chelsea, Michigan

Some artwork by Jennifer Craig used with permission.

Library of Congress Cataloging-in-Publication Data

Catalog record is available from the Library of Congress

ISBN 1-57504-059-X

ANN ARBOR PRESS, INC.
121 South Main Street, Chelsea, Michigan 48118

Printed in the United States of America
1 2 3 4 5 6 7 8 9 0

Introduction

Mathematics is the key to many of the most important aspects of a golf course superintendent's profession. Budgeting, fertilizer and pesticide application, the ordering and application of topdressing, irrigation, and many other important parts of golf course operation require a thorough understanding of basic mathematical principles and the ability to relate those principles to real-world situations.

The purpose of this book is to offer examples of the types of mathematical problems that face golf course superintendents and to provide practical methods of solving these problems. Each chapter contains additional practice problems that can be used as a self test to evaluate your understanding of the material. Answers to the practice problems and detailed descriptions of how they are solved can be found in Appendix B.

Table of Contents

1. Area Measurement Calculations 1

2. Volume Calculations 19

3. Fertilizer Calculations 35

4. Pesticide Calculations 57

5. Spreader and Sprayer Calibration 75

6. Irrigation Calculations 109

7. Seeding Rate Calculations 119

Appendix A. Conversion Factors 125

Appendix B. Answers to Problems 129

Index 149

Area Measurement Calculations

Area measurements are the first calculations that any turfgrass manager should learn. It is important for the golf course superintendent to be able to calculate area accurately, whether it is to topdress greens, fertilize fairways, or overseed tees. Accurate area calculations can save money and time, as well as help prevent misapplication of pesticides.

Area is defined in terms of square measures. The most commonly used area measurements are square feet (ft^2) and acres (ac). Greens and tees are commonly measured in units of 1,000 ft^2, and fairways and roughs are measured in acres.

Calculating area can be accomplished using several methods, including geometric figure calculations, offset determination, and radius method.

GEOMETRIC FIGURES

Most calculations for surface area can be done using geometric figures. The five basic geometric figures include rectangles or squares, trapezoids, triangles, circles, and ovals.

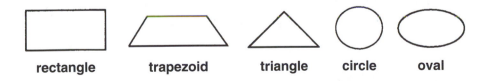

| rectangle | trapezoid | triangle | circle | oval |

Many larger irregularly shaped areas can be segmented into smaller geometric figures.

For example, the two shapes below can easily be transformed into a series of smaller shapes.

2 rectangles   **2 triangles + 1 rectangle**

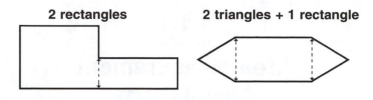

Rectangle

A rectangle is a parallelogram with four right angles. The area of a rectangle is found by multiplying the length (l) by the width (w).

Area = (l)(w)

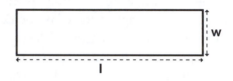

Example 1.1

Determine the area of a rectangle where l = 100 ft and w = 50 ft.

Area = (l)(w)
Area = (100 ft)(50 ft)
      = 5,000 ft^2

Trapezoid

A trapezoid is a quadrilateral with only two parallel sides. The area is found by multiplying the average length of the parallel sides (A and B) by the height (h).

$$\text{Area} = \left(\frac{A+B}{2}\right)(h)$$

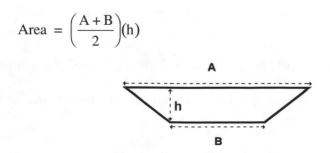

Example 1.2

Determine the area of a trapezoid where a = 200 ft, b = 300 ft, and h = 50 ft.

Area = [(a + b)/2]h
Area = [(200 ft + 300 ft)/2](50 ft)
       = [500 ft/2](50 ft)
       = (250 ft)(50 ft)
       = 12,500 ft^2

Triangle

A triangle is a polygon with three sides. The area of a triangle is one-half the base (b) multiplied by the height (h).

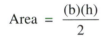

$$\text{Area} = \frac{(b)(h)}{2}$$

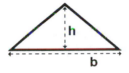

Example 1.3

Determine the area of a triangle where b = 200 ft and h = 100 ft.

Area = [(b)(h)]/2
Area = [(200 ft)(100 ft)]/2
       = 20,000 ft^2/2
       = 10,000 ft^2

Circle

A circle is a closed curve of which every point on the edge of the curve is equidistant from a fixed point within the curve. The area of a circle is the radius squared (r^2) multiplied by 3.14. The radius is equal to one-half the diameter of the circle. The numerical value for pi (π) is 3.14.

Area = $(3.14)r^2$

Example 1.4

Determine the area of a circle where r = 100 ft.

Area = $(3.14)(100 \text{ ft})^2$
    = $31,400 \text{ ft}^2$

Oval

An oval has an elliptical or egg-like shape. The area of an oval is the length (l) multiplied by the width (w), multiplied by 0.8.

Area = $[(l)(w)](0.8)$

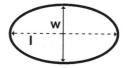

Example 1.5

Determine the area of an oval where w = 50 ft and l = 100 ft.

Area = $[(50 \text{ ft})(100 \text{ ft})](0.8)$
    = $4,000 \text{ ft}^2$

Problem 1.1

Using the geometric method of determining area, determine the area of the green (A), fairway (B+ C+ D) and tee (E) for the 435-yard par-4 hole. All necessary dimensions are noted on the figure below.

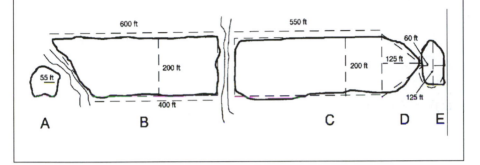

Problem 1.1

Section A - Green (circle) r = 55 ft

Section B - Fairway (trapezoid)

Section C - Fairway (rectangle)

Section D - Fairway (triangle)

Total of fairway area (B+ C+ D)

Section E - Tee (oval) l = 125 ft; w = 60 ft

(See Appendix B for answers.)

OFFSET METHOD

The offset method is used to measure irregularly shaped areas. It reduces large areas to a series of smaller trapezoids that are equally spaced along a measured line. This method will determine the area to within 5%.

The four steps in determining area by the offset method are as follows:

Step 1. Determine the length line. This is the longest axis of the figure. Its endpoints should be labeled A and B.

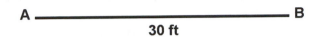

A ——————————————— B
30 ft

Step 2. Mark offset lines at right angles (90°) to the length line. Choose how many offset lines to use so that they divide line AB into equal segments and define regions amenable to calculation. For example, if the length line were 60 ft, a logical distance between offset lines would be 10 ft, since 60 divided by 10 equals 6, a whole number. If the length line is 300 ft or more, intervals of 10 to 30 yd should be used. If the shape of the area is uniform, then fewer offset lines are needed. However, if the shape of the area is irregular, more offset lines are needed. To ensure accuracy, use as many offset lines as possible.

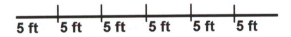

5 ft   5 ft   5 ft   5 ft   5 ft   5 ft

Step 3. Measure the length of each offset line. These are measured from one edge of the area to the other.

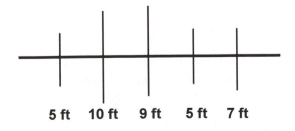

5 ft   10 ft   9 ft   5 ft   7 ft

Step 4. Add up the lengths of all offset lines and multiply by the distance between offset lines on the length line.

$$5 + 10 + 9 + 5 + 7 = 36 \text{ ft}$$

$$(36 \text{ ft})(5 \text{ ft}) = 180 \text{ ft}^2$$

Example 1.6

Using the offset method, determine the area of a sand bunker.

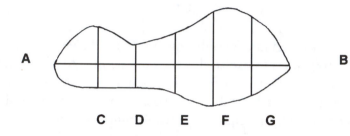

Step 1. Determine the length line.
 The distance between points A and B is 60 ft.

Step 2. Offset lines will be set every 10 ft.

Step 3. The lengths of the offset lines are as follows:

  C = 15 ft
  D = 10 ft
  E = 15 ft
  F = 25 ft
  G = 20 ft
 Total = 85 ft

Step 4. The total length of the combined offset lines is 85 ft.
 The distance between offset lines is 10 ft.

  area = (85 ft)(10 ft)
  area = 850 ft^2

Problem 1.2

Using the offset method, determine the area of a 330-yard fairway. The distance between offset lines is 30 yards.

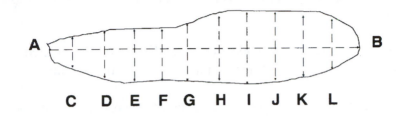

The lengths of the offset lines are as follows:

C = 30 yd   D = 55 yd   E = 60 yd
F = 60 yd   G = 70 yd   H = 80 yd
I = 80 yd   J = 70 yd   K = 60 yd
L = 55 yd

MODIFIED OFFSET METHOD

Some areas, such as ponds and lakes, cannot be measured using the conventional offset method. However, they can be measured by a variation of it. The steps in determining area by the modified offset method are as follows:

Step 1. Construct a rectangle around the figure to be measured. Label the corners A, B, C, and D. Determine the length line (l) and the width (w).

The length line (l) equals the distance between point A and B, or C and D.

The overall width (w) equals the distance between point A and C, or B and D.

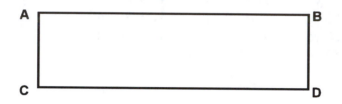

Step 2. Mark offset lines from each length line to the closest perimeter of the measured area. Each offset will have two lines (E1 + E2, F1 + F2, etc.).

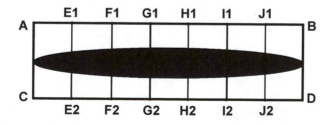

Step 3. Determine the lengths of the offset lines by measuring from the outside edge to the edge of the pond and add the paired offset lines together.

$$(E1 + E2 = E), (F1 + F2 = F), \text{etc.}$$

Step 4. Subtract the sum of each pair of offset lines from the overall width. The results are the distances across the irregular figure along each offset line.

Step 5. Total all of those results

Step 6. Multiply the total by the distance between offset lines.

Example 1.7

Using the modified offset method, determine the area of the following.

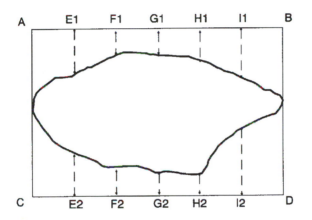

Step 1. Construct rectangle. The length (from point A to B or C to D) = 60 ft. The width (from point A to C or B to D) = 40 ft.

Step 2. Offset lines are spaced every 10 ft.

Step 3: The lengths of the offset lines are as follows:

E1 = 10 ft	F1 = 6 ft	G1 = 6 ft	H1 = 8 ft	I1 = 12 ft
E2 = 10 ft	F2 = 6 ft	G2 = 4 ft	H2 = 4 ft	I2 = 16 ft
E = 20 ft	F = 12 ft	G = 10 ft	H = 12 ft	I = 28 ft

Step 4. Next, subtract the value of the offset lines from 40 ft and total.

E	$40 - 20 = 20$ ft
F	$40 - 12 = 28$ ft
G	$40 - 10 = 30$ ft
H	$40 - 12 = 28$ ft
I	$40 - 28 = 12$ ft
Total	118 ft

Step 5. Multiply the total by the distance between the offset lines.

$$(118 \text{ ft})(10 \text{ ft}) = 1{,}180 \text{ ft}^2$$

Problem 1.3

Using the modified offset method, determine the area of the pond in the figure below.

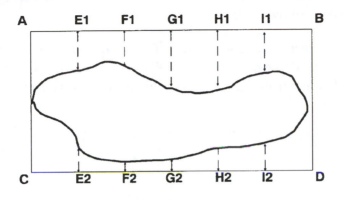

Offset lines are as follows:

Length line = 60 yd; the overall width = 30 yd.
The distance between offset lines is 10 yd.

E1 = 9 yd   F1 = 10 yd   G1 = 13 yd   H1 = 13 yd   I1 = 10 yd
E2 = 6 yd   F2 = 3 yd   G2 = 4 yd   H2 = 5 yd   I2 = 9 yd

AVERAGE RADIUS METHOD

A final method used to measure irregularly shaped circular areas is to convert the area into a circle. This is done by determining the average radius of the area. The steps in determining area by the average radius method are as follows.

Step 1. Construct a template out of a 4-ft by 4-ft piece of plywood. Mark the center of the plywood with 2 lines that make 4 right angles (90°). Next, mark a line from the centerpoint to the edge every 10°.

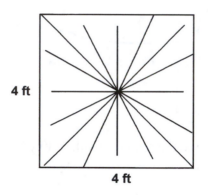

Step 2. Locate a central point within the area to be measured. Place the template on this spot and measure the distance from the central point to the edge of the area. Make 18 to 36 measurements every 10° to 20°.

Step 3. Total all of the radius measurements and divide by the number of measurements. This equals the average radius (r). For example, if the 36 radius measurements totaled 1,800 ft, you would divide 36 into 1,800 to obtain the average radius. 1800/36 = 50 ft

Step 4. Calculate the area of the circle using the average radius. Area = 3.14r^2.

$$A = (3.14)(50 \text{ ft})^2 = 7850 \text{ ft}^2$$

Example 1.8

Using the average radius method, determine the area of the following.

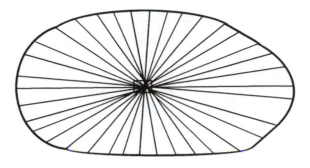

Step 1. Make 36 measurements every 10°.

Step 2. Total the radius measurement.

Total = 1,680 ft

Step 3. Divide the total of the measurements by 36.

1,680 ft/36 = 46.7 ft = average radius

Step 4. Determine the area of a circle using the average radius.

Area = $(3.14)(46.7 \text{ ft})^2$
Area = $(3.14)(2180.9 \text{ ft})^2$
Area = $6,848 \text{ ft}^2$

The collar area can be determined by extending the 36 measurements to the other edge of the collar. To determine collar area, first calculate the combined collar-green area and then subtract the total green area from this value.

Example 1.9

Determine the area of the collar on the green in Example 1.8.

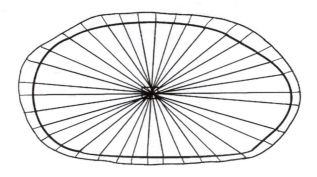

Step 1. Make 36 measurements every 10° as in Example 1.8, but also include the collar in all radius calculations.

Step 2. Total the measurement.

total for collar + green = 1,875 ft
total for green   = 1,680 ft

Step 3. Divide the total of the measurements by 36.

1,875 ft/36 = 52.1 ft = average radius of collar + green
1,680 ft /36 = 46.7 ft = average radius of green

Step 4. Determine the area of a circle using the average radius.

collar + green
Area = $(3.14)(52.1 \text{ ft})^2 = 8,523.3 \text{ ft}^2$

green only
Area = $(3.14)(46.7 \text{ ft})^2 = 6,848 \text{ ft}^2$

Step 5. Determine the area of the collar by subtracting the green only value from the collar + green value.

$8,523.3 \text{ ft}^2 - 6848 \text{ ft}^2 = 1675.3 \text{ ft}^2$ of collar

Problem 1.4

Using the average radius method, determine the area of a green and collar that have the following dimensions:

collar + green = 36 radius measurements of 2,250 ft
green = 36 radius measurements of 2,025 ft

2

Volume Calculations

The golf course superintendent needs to be able to calculate volume in order to properly apply topdressing to greens, apply pesticides, or determine the volume of water in a pond.

Volume is defined in terms of cubic measures. A cubic measure is a unit multiplied by a similar unit, and then multiplied by another similar unit (example: ft × ft × ft = ft³). Common means of expressing volume are cubic yards (yd³), cubic feet (ft³) and gallons (gal). Cubic yards is a common measurement for sand and topdressing volumes, and cubic feet and gallons are common volume measurements for liquids.

The first step in calculating volume is to determine the surface area. In Chapter 1, the surface area was calculated by several methods. When the height of the area being determined is equal over the entire area, volume is calculated by multiplying surface area (A) by height (h).

$$Volume = (A)(h)$$

GEOMETRIC FIGURES

Two common shapes of this type are the cube and the cylinder.

Cube

The volume of the cube is calculated by determining the area of a rectangle (see Example 1.1) and multiplying by the height (h).

$$Volume = (l)(w)(h)$$

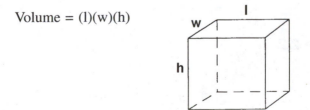

Example 2.1

width = 30 ft
length = 20 ft
height = 5 ft

Step 1. Determine the area of the rectangle by multiplying the length by the width.

Area = (20 ft)(30 ft)
Area = 600 ft^2

Step 2. Determine the volume of the cube by multiplying the area by the height.

Volume = (600 ft^2)5 ft
Volume = 3,000 ft^3

Cylinder

The volume of the cylinder is calculated by first determining the area of a circle (see Example 1.4) and multiplying by the height (h).

$$Volume = [3.14(r^2)]h$$

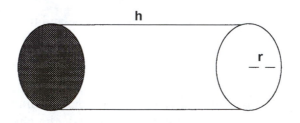

Example 2.2

r = 5 ft
h = 10 ft

Step 1. Determine the area of a circle by squaring the radius and multiplying by 3.14.

$$\text{Area} = (3.14)(5\ \text{ft})^2$$
$$= 78.5\ \text{ft}^2$$

Step 2. Determine the volume of a cylinder by multiplying the area by the height.

$$\text{Volume} = (78.5\ \text{ft}^2)10\ \text{ft}$$
$$= 785\ \text{ft}^3$$

If the height of the volume being determined is not equal over the entire area, special steps need to be taken to determine volume. The most commonly used shape to calculate this type of area is the cone.

Cone

The volume of a cone is calculated by determining the area of a circle or base and multiplying by the height (h) and dividing by 3.

$$\text{Volume} = \frac{(3.14)(r^2)(h)}{3}$$

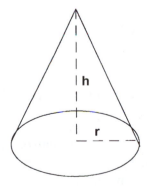

Example 2.3

r = 10 ft
h = 5 ft

Step 1. Determine the area of a circle as in Example 2.2.

$$\begin{aligned} \text{Area} &= (3.14)(10 \text{ ft})^2 \\ &= (3.14)(100 \text{ ft}^2) \\ &= 314 \text{ ft}^2 \end{aligned}$$

Step 2. Determine the volume of the cone by multiplying the area by the height and dividing by 3.

$$\begin{aligned} \text{Volume} &= (314 \text{ ft}^2)(5 \text{ ft})/3 \\ &= (1570 \text{ ft}^3)/3 \\ &= 523.3 \text{ ft}^3 \end{aligned}$$

Irregular Shapes

If the height of the area being measured is irregular, it is necessary to determine the average height by making 15 to 30 measurements. The average is then used as h in the calculation:

irregular cube: Volume = (l)(w)(h)

irregular cylinder: Volume = $(3.14)(r^2)(h)$

irregular cone: Volume = $\dfrac{(3.14)(r^2)(h)}{3}$

MEASURING THE VOLUME OF TOPDRESSING, SAND, OR SOIL

There are 27 ft^3 in 1 yd^3. To visualize how much 1 yd^3 is, take 27 boxes that measure 1 ft by 1 ft by 1 ft and stack them in rows of 3. To convert the 3,000 ft^3 volume in Example 2.1 into cubic yard, it is necessary to divide by 27.

$$3{,}000 \text{ ft}^3 \div 27 \text{ ft}^3/\text{yd}^3 = 111.1 \text{ yd}^3$$

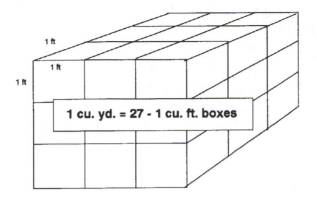

1 ft

1 ft

1 ft

1 cu. yd. = 27 - 1 cu. ft. boxes

The height of many areas that are measured on golf courses is in inches rather than feet. This is especially true when calculating topdressing needs. The figure below shows the comparison of 1/8-in. topdressing on a 4-in. soil profile. It is necessary to convert inches into feet before calculating volume. There are 1,728 in.^{3} in 1 ft^3.

1/8-inch topdressing

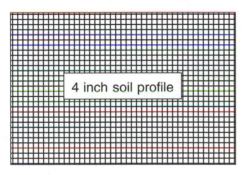

4 inch soil profile

To help visualize the volume of topdress material needed for topdressing, imagine that you are standing in a room that measures 12 ft by 20 ft, and you fill the room up with topdress material to a 1-ft depth.

How much topdress material would be needed?

This calculation is fairly simple, since the calculations will be made in feet. First, calculate the surface area of the room by multiplying 12 ft by 20 ft.

$$12 \text{ ft} \times 20 \text{ ft} = 240 \text{ ft}^2$$

Next, the volume is calculated by multiplying the surface area (240 ft^2) by the 1-ft depth.

$$240 \text{ ft}^2 \times 1 \text{ ft} = 240 \text{ ft}^3$$

For topdress on a golf green, the units of measurement are in fractions of an inch, not feet. Therefore, it is necessary to first convert from inches to feet in order to calculate volume. The following examples should help you understand this process fully.

Example 2.4

A basic question in the purchase of topdressing material would be the following. How much topdressing material would be needed to topdress a 6,500-ft^2 green to a depth of 1/16 in. and 1/4 in.?

To solve this problem, first convert the topdress depth from inches to feet. Next, multiply the depth (in feet) by the square footage of the green. This yields the volume of topdress material in ft^3. Finally, convert ft^3 to yd^3 by dividing by 27/ft^3/yd^3.

Topdress depth of 1/16 in.

(a)   h = 1/16 in. depth = 1 ÷ 16 = 0.0625 in.
  = 0.0625 in. ÷ 12 in./ft
  = 0.0052 ft

Volume = 6,500 ft^2 × 0.0052 ft
  = 33.8 ft^3

Note: If 1 yd^3 = 27 ft^3, then (X) yd^3 = 33.8 ft^3

X yd^3 = 33.8 ft^3 ÷ 27 ft^3/yd^3
  = 1.25 yd^3

Topdress depth of 1/4 in.

(b)   h = 1/4 in. depth = 1 ÷ 4 = 0.25 in.
  = 0.25 in. ÷ 12 in./ft
  = 0.021 ft

Volume = 6,500 ft^2 × 0.021 ft
  = 136.5 ft^3

Note: If 1 yd^3 = 27 ft^3, then (X) yd^3 = 136.5 ft^3

X yd^3 = 136.5 ft^3 ÷ 27 ft^3/yd^3
  = 5.0 yd^3

Once the amount of topdressing material has been determined for 1/16-in. depth, the amount of topdress material for the 1/4-in. depth can be determined by cross-multiplication.

a. $\dfrac{X \text{ yd}^3}{0.25 \text{ in.}} = \dfrac{1.25 \text{ yd}^3}{0.0625 \text{ in.}}$

b. $X \text{ yd}^3 = \dfrac{(1.25 \text{ yd}^3)(0.25 \text{ in.})}{0.0625 \text{ in.}}$

c. $X \text{ yd}^3 = \dfrac{0.3125 \text{ yd}^3 \text{ - in.}}{0.0625 \text{ in.}}$

d. $X = 5 \text{ yd}^3$

Example 2.5

It is also very common for a green to be aerified before being topdressed. If the topdress material were applied based solely on the depth of topdress and the surface area of the green, then the amount applied would be insufficient to provide a uniform layer while filling the aeration holes. Therefore it is important to determine the volume that would be created by the aeration hole before ordering topdress material.

Step 1. The first step is to determine the total volume of all core holes for 1 ft^2. If the aeration creates 27 holes per ft^2 with a core diameter of 1/2 in. (radius = 0.5 ÷ 2 = 0.25 in.) and a depth of 3 in., then what is the volume of all core holes in 1 ft^2?

Surface Area of 1 core = $3.14(r^2)$
= $3.14(0.25 \text{ in.})^2$
= $3.14(0.0625 \text{ in.}^2)$
= 0.19625 in.^2
Volume of 1 core = Area(h)
= $0.19625 \text{ in.}^2 (3 \text{ in.})$
= $0.59 \text{ in.}^3/\text{hole}$
Volume of cores per ft^2 = $0.59 \text{ in.}^3 (27 \text{ holes/ft}^2)$
= $15.9 \text{ in.}^3/\text{ft}^2$

Step 2. Using the value calculated above, how much topdressing material would be needed to fill the core holes for a 6,500-ft^2 green?

This problem can be solved by converting the volume of core holes for 1 ft^2 from in.^{3} to ft^3 and multiplying by the surface area of green. This will yield the volume of topdress material necessary to fill all core holes for the green in ft^3. Then, convert the total volume of topdress from ft^3 to yd^3 by dividing by 27.

To convert in.^{3} of topdress to ft^3 of topdress divide by 1,728 (in.^{3}/ft^3).

$$X\ ft^3 = 15.9\ in.^3 \div 1,728\ in.^3/ft^3$$
$$= 0.0092\ ft^3/ft^2$$

To calculate the total amount of topdress material, multiply the volume (ft^3)/ft^2 by the square footage of the green.

$$\text{Volume in } ft^3 = (0.0092\ ft^3/ft^2)(6,500\ ft^2)$$
$$= 59.8\ ft^3$$

To convert the volume of topdress for the green from ft^3 to yd^3, divide by 27.

$$\text{Volume in } yd^3 = 59.8\ ft^3 \div 27\ ft^3/yd^3$$
$$= 2.21\ yd^3$$

Problem 2.1

How much topdressing material is needed to cover a 9,200-ft^2 green to the following depths? (Put all answers in yd^3/green.)

a) to topdress to a 1/32-in. depth?

b) to topdress to a 3/8-in. depth?

c) to fill 3/4-in.-diameter × 3.5-in.-deep core holes? (36 holes/ft^2)

Often, topdress material is stored in bins or piles, without any idea of the volume on hand in storage. If the topdress material is to be used, it becomes necessary to calculate the volume of the stored topdress material to determine how much area can be topdressed.

Example 2.6

(1) How many ft^2 of green can be topdressed to 1/4-in. depth with a quantity of topdress material that is stored in a 20-ft by 15-ft rectangular bin that measures a level 7 ft high?

To solve this problem, first determine the best method for determining volume. This is a rectangular-shaped pile of topdress material, thus the calculation of a cube should suffice to determine the volume of the pile.

(a) First, determine the surface area of the pile.

$$\text{Surface area of the topdress pile} = 20 \text{ ft} \times 15 \text{ ft}$$
$$= 300 \text{ ft}^2$$

(b) Second, determine the volume of the pile in ft^3.

$$\text{Volume of cube} = \text{surface area} \times h$$
$$= 300 \text{ ft}^2 \times 7 \text{ ft}$$
$$= 2,100 \text{ ft}^3$$

(c) Third, convert the volume for ft^3 to yd^3

$$= 2,100 \text{ ft}^3 \div 27 \text{ ft}^3/\text{yd}^3$$
$$= 77.8 \text{ yd}^3$$

(d) Next, determine how many yd^3 are needed to topdress 1 ft^2 to a 1/4-in. depth.

$$h = 1/4\text{-in. depth} = 1 \div 4 = 0.25 \text{ in.}$$
$$= 0.25 \text{ in.} \div 12 \text{ in./ft}$$
$$= 0.021 \text{ ft}$$
$$\text{Volume for 1 ft}^2 = 0.021 \text{ ft} \times 1 \text{ ft}^2$$
$$= 0.021 \text{ ft}^3/\text{ft}^2$$
$$= 0.021 \div 27$$
$$= 0.00078 \text{ yd}^3/\text{ft}^2$$

(e) Finally, to determine how much surface area the pile of topdress material will cover, divide the total volume in Part c above by the yd^3/ft^2 in Part d.

If it takes 0.00078 yd^3 of topdress material to cover 1 ft^2, then 77.8 yd^3 will cover X ft^2.

$$\frac{0.00078 \text{ yd}^3}{1 \text{ ft}^2} = \frac{77.8 \text{ yd}^3}{X \text{ ft}^2}$$

$$77.8 \text{ yd}^3 \div 0.00078 \text{ yd}^3/\text{ft}^2 = 99{,}743.6 \text{ ft}^2$$

(2) How many ft^2 of green can be topdressed to 3/8-in. depth with a topdress material pile (cone-shaped) that measures 5 ft high and has a diameter of 30 ft?

To solve this problem, first determine the best method for determining volume. This is a cone-shaped pile of topdress material, thus the calculation of a cone should suffice to determine the volume of the pile.

$$\text{Radius (r)} = 30 \text{ ft} \div 2$$
$$= 15 \text{ ft}$$
$$\text{Height (h)} = 5 \text{ ft}$$

(a) First, determine the surface area of the pile.

$$\begin{aligned}\text{Surface area of the topdress pile} &= (3.14)(r^2)\\ &= (3.14)(15 \text{ ft})^2\\ &= (3.14)(225 \text{ ft}^2)\\ &= 706.5 \text{ ft}^2\end{aligned}$$

(b) Second, determine the volume of the pile in ft^3.

$$\begin{aligned}\text{Volume of cone} &= [(\text{surface area})(h)]/3\\ &= [(706.5 \text{ ft}^2)(5 \text{ ft})]/3\\ &= 3{,}532.5 \text{ ft}^3/3\\ &= 1{,}177.5 \text{ ft}^3\end{aligned}$$

(c) Third, convert the volume for ft^3 to yd^3.

$$\begin{aligned}&= 1{,}177.5 \text{ ft}^3 \div 27 \text{ ft}^3/\text{yd}^3\\ &= 43.6 \text{ yd}^3\end{aligned}$$

(d) Next, determine how many yd^3 are needed to topdress 1 ft to a 3/8-in. depth.

$$\begin{aligned}\text{h} = 3/8\text{-in. depth} &= 3 \div 8 = 0.375 \text{ in.}\\ &= 0.375 \text{ in.} \div 12 \text{ in./ft}\\ &= 0.03125 \text{ ft}\\ \text{Volume for 1 ft}^2 &= 0.03125 \text{ ft}(1 \text{ ft}^2)\\ &= 0.03125 \text{ ft}^3/\text{ft}^2\end{aligned}$$

$$= 0.03125 \div 27$$
$$= 0.00116 \text{ yd}^3/\text{ft}^2$$

(e) Finally, to determine how much surface area the pile of topdress material will cover, divide the total volume in Part c by the yd^3/ft^2 in Part d.

If it takes 0.00116 yd of topdress material to cover 1 ft^2, then 43.6 yd^3 will cover X ft^2.

$$\frac{0.00116 \text{ yd}^3}{1 \text{ ft}^2} = \frac{43.6 \text{ yd}^3}{X \text{ ft}^2}$$

43.6 yd^3 $\div$ 0.00116 yd^3/ft^2 = 37,586.2 ft^2

Problem 2.2

How many ft^2 of green can be topdressed to 1/8-in. depth with sand that is stored in a rectangular storage bin that measures 15 ft by 20 ft? The average height of the sand is 6 ft.

Problem 2.3

How much sand, peat, and soil would you order to mix a 7-2-1 mix when topdressing at 3/8 in. to cover 126,000 ft^2?

Remember, 7-2-1 is equivalent to 70-20-10.

MEASURING THE VOLUME OF LIQUIDS

There are 7.4805 gal of water in 1 ft^3 of water. To convert ft^3 into gal, multiple ft^3 by 7.4805.

Example 2.7

A pond has a surface area of 20,000 ft^2, and a average depth of 25 ft. What is the volume of water in the pond?

It is first necessary to calculate the volume of the pond in ft^3. Then convert this volume from ft^3 to gallons by multiplying the volume in ft^3 by 7.4805.

(1) Calculate the volume of the pond in ft^3.

$$20,000 \text{ ft}^2 \times 25 \text{ ft} = 500,000 \text{ ft}^3$$

(2) Convert the volume from ft^3 to gal by multiplying the volume in ft^3 by 7.4805.

$$\frac{7.4805 \text{ gal}}{1 \text{ ft}^3} = \frac{X \text{ gal}}{500,000 \text{ ft}^3}$$

$$500,000 \text{ ft}^3 \times 7.4805 \text{ gal/ft}^3 = X \text{ gal} = 3,740,250 \text{ gal}$$

Problem 2.3

A pond has a surface area of 1 ac and an average depth of 75 ft. What is the volume of water in the pond?

3

Fertilizer Calculations

The calculations involved in the application of fertilizers are a necessary part of a superintendent's job. They are a critical part of the budgeting process and they play an important role in everyday management procedures. The first step in comprehending fertilizer calculations is to understand some of the terminology associated with fertilizer materials.

Ratio refers to the relative quantities of the nutrients. A 10-10-10 fertilizer has a ratio of 1-1-1, as would a 20-20-20. A 20-5-10 fertilizer has a ratio of 4-1-2. Ratio provides little information about the actual amount of nutrients in the container. It is the analysis that provides the information needed to perform fertilizer calculations.

Analysis refers to the percentage by weight of the fertilizer nutrients. The analysis will be listed on the container, either in prominent numbers across the front of the package, or as a part of the label. Nitrogen (N) is expressed on an elemental basis, whereas phosphorus (P) and potassium (K) are expressed as phosphoric acid (P_2O_5) and potash (K_2O). A 10-10-10 fertilizer contains by weight 10% N, 10% P_2O_5 and 10% K_2O. A 100-lb bag would contain 10 lb N, 10 lb P_2O_5 and 10 lb K_2O.

A frequent mistake is to interpret the analysis as though the last two numbers referred to percentage by weight of elemental P and K This can lead to large errors, and care should be taken that the following conversions are always used when fertilizer calculations involving P and K are made:

P_2O_5 contains 44% P

K_2O contains 83% K

Example 3.1

A 50-lb bag of fertilizer has an analysis of 20-5-10. How much N, P, and K does this bag contain?

The analysis lists the percentage by weight of N, P_2O_5, and K_2O. First determine the amount of these materials by multiplying the percentage of each of the materials by the total weight of the fertilizer in the bag.

1) $(50 \text{ lb})(0.20) = 10 \text{ lb N}$
2) $(50 \text{ lb})(0.05) = 2.5 \text{ lb } P_2O_5$
3) $(50 \text{ lb})(0.10) = 5 \text{ lb } K_2O$

The amount of elemental N has been calculated to be 10 lb, but another step will be required to determine the amount of P and K.

4) $(2.5 \text{ lb } P_2O_5)(0.44) = 1.1 \text{ lb P}$
5) $(5 \text{ lb } K_2O)(0.83) = 4.15 \text{ lb K}$

The bag contains 10 lb of N, 1.1 lb of P and 4.15 lb of K.

Problem 3.1

How many lb of N, P, and K are there in a ton (2,000 lb) of a 23-3-15 fertilizer?

Problem 3.2

How many lb of N, P, and K are there in a partially filled bag of a 15-5-10 fertilizer that contains 38 lb of material?

HOW MUCH FERTILIZER TO APPLY

A second, more useful type of calculation is that required to determine how much fertilizer needs to be applied to a certain area to deliver the required amount of fertilizer elements.

The calculation required to solve this type of problem often proves to be very confusing to those just beginning to learn about fertilizer application.

With a little logic, some simple drawings, a little mathematics, and some practice, however, this type of problem can be easily solved.

Two methods of working these problems will be presented. They are basically the same, but involve a different approach in the thought process. Some people are more comfortable with the first process and some are more comfortable with the second. Choose the method that is best for you.

Method 1

The first method involves some simple algebra. This is the preferred method of the two because it provides a rapid approach to working more complex problems. It is a logical approach that will help you think your way through the multiple-step problems that often face the golf course superintendent in the budgeting process. Method 1 will be used in the examples presented in this book.

Example 3.2

How much 20-5-15 fertilizer would have to be applied to 1,000 ft^2 of green to deliver 1 lb of N per 1,000 ft^2?

First, look at the problem and think about it. One pound of N is needed per 1,000 ft^2. The material is only 20% N by weight; therefore, more than one lb of the fertilizer will be needed to provide the 1 lb of N. The problem is, how much more?

Begin by drawing a block to represent the 1 lb N.

1 lb N

Next, draw a dotted line to represent the amount of fertilizer that would need to be applied to provide this 1 lb of N. It is known that more than 1 lb of 20-5-15 is needed to provide the 1 lb of N, but the exact amount is not known at this time. Label this total amount of fertilizer X to signify that it is some unknown amount.

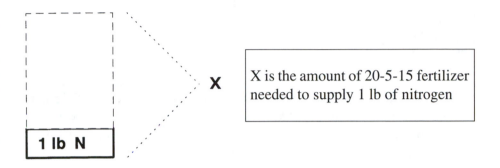

X is the amount of 20-5-15 fertilizer needed to supply 1 lb of nitrogen

Now go back one step. If there were a known amount of 20-5-15—let's say 10 lb in a container—it would be an easy matter to determine the amount of N in the container.

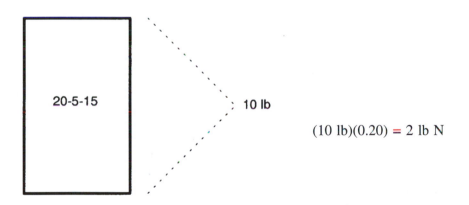

$$(10 \text{ lb})(0.20) = 2 \text{ lb N}$$

Simply multiply the 0.20 (20%) times the 10 lb of fertilizer. The answer is 2 lb N.

In Example 3.2, the amount of N is already known: 1 lb of N is needed. It is the total amount of fertilizer needed to achieve that amount of N that is unknown. The concept involved in working the two problems, however, is exactly the same.

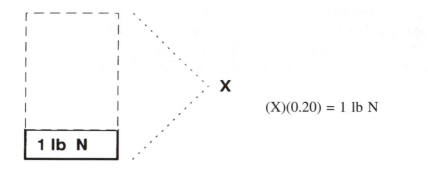

$$(X)(0.20) = 1 \text{ lb N}$$

The X in this problem stands for an unknown amount of 20-5-15 that will have to be applied to 1,000 ft² to apply 1 lb of N per 1,000 ft². In solving this problem, it is known that 20 percent of some unknown amount of fertilizer (X) contains 1 lb of N. It may be useful to say the following words to help understand the problem: "Twenty percent of some amount of 20-5-10 fertilizer will be just enough to provide 1 lb of N." By solving this mathematical relationship, that unknown quantity of fertilizer can be determined.

This is done by dividing through by 0.20, as follows:

$$\frac{(X)(\cancel{0.20})}{\cancel{0.20}} = \frac{1}{0.20}$$

$$X = \frac{1}{0.20}$$

$$X = 5 \text{ lb}$$

To solve this problem with a calculator, simply put a 1 in the calculator and divide by 0.20. The answer is 5 lb of the fertilizer. It has now been calculated that if 5 lb of 20-5-15 fertilizer is applied to 1,000 ft² of green, 1 lb of N will have been applied.

The answer can be checked easily by answering one additional question. If 5 lb of 20-5-15 fertilizer were to be applied to 1,000 ft² of green, how much N would be applied?

$$(5 \text{ lb})(0.20) = 1 \text{ lb N}$$

The answer checks, and the proper amount of fertilizer (5 lb) has been determined.

This is usually not the end of the problem, however. Fertilizer calculations are generally made on the basis of 1,000 ft², but in the real world several thousand square feet usually are involved. To take the problem this extra step will require one additional mathematical relationship.

Example 3.3

How much 18-5-9 fertilizer would have to be purchased to apply 0.75 lb of N per 1,000 ft² to 55,000 ft² of greens?

First, determine how much fertilizer will be required per 1,000 ft², as was done in Example 3.2. It is known that 0.75 lb N is required; the question is how much 18-5-9 has to be applied to 1,000 ft² to deliver that 0.75 lb N?

Always begin by first setting up the problem properly.

1) $(X)(0.18) = 0.75$ lb N

Then say to yourself, "Eighteen percent of some amount of 18-5-9 (X) will provide 0.75 lb of N." Next, solve the problem by dividing 0.75 by 0.18. Put 0.75 in the calculator and divide it by 0.18. The answer is 4.166, which can be rounded to 4.2 lb of 18-5-9.

2) $X = \dfrac{0.75}{0.18}$

3) $X = 4.2$ lb 18-5-9

A total of 4.2 lb 18-5-9 fertilizer will be needed for each 1,000 ft² of green to apply a rate of 0.75 lb N per 1,000 ft².

The next part of the question is, how much 18-5-9 will be needed to treat 55,000 ft²?

This is most easily calculated with a mathematical proportion, which is arranged as follows:

$$\frac{4.2 \text{ lb}}{1,000 \text{ ft}^2} = \frac{X \text{ lb}}{55,000 \text{ ft}^2}$$

In solving this problem, recite the following words: "If 4.2 lb of 18-5-9 is required per 1,000 ft^2, how much (X) 18-5-9 will be required to treat 55,000 ft^2?"

This type of mathematical relationship is solved by cross-multiplying and dividing:

$$(X)(1,000) = (4.2)(55,000)$$

$$(X)(1,000) = 231,000$$

$$X = \frac{231,000}{1,000}$$

$$X = 231 \text{ lb of } 18\text{-}5\text{-}9$$

It has now been determined that 231 lb of 18-5-9 fertilizer will be needed to treat 55,000 ft^2 of greens at a N rate of 0.75 lb per 1,000 ft^2.

Problem 3.3

How much 15-3-10 fertilizer would be needed to apply 1 lb N per 1,000 ft^2 to 170,000 ft^2 of greens?

Problem 3.4

How much 17-5-10 fertilizer would be needed to apply 0.75 lb of N per 1,000 ft^2 to 40 ac of golf course fairways? (1 ac = 43,560 ft^2)

Method 2

Now let's look at a little different approach to solving these problems.

Example 3.4

The second method of working these problems is to base everything on 100 lb of fertilizer.

In Example 3.3, we have an 18-5-9 fertilizer. This material is 18% N, which means that every 100 lb of it contains 18 lb N. We want to apply 0.75 lb N to every 1,000 ft^2.

The problem could be set up using the following logic.

If 100 lb of 18-5-9 contains 18 lb of N, how many pounds would be needed to apply 0.75 lb N? Write this mathematically as follows:

$$\frac{100 \text{ lb}}{18 \text{ lb N}} = \frac{X \text{ lb fertilizer}}{0.75 \text{ lb N}}$$

Next, cross-multiply and divide.

$$(18)(X) = (100)(0.75)$$

$$X = \frac{75}{18}$$

$$X = 4.2 \text{ lb of } 18\text{-}5\text{-}9$$

The answer is exactly the same.

The second part of the problem is worked exactly as it was in Example 3.3 and the final answer is 231 lb of fertilizer are needed for the 55,000 ft^2.

CALCULATIONS FOR ELEMENTS OTHER THAN N

There will be times when nutrients other than N will be of primary interest. When that is the case, the principles involved in the calculation are the same, but there may be an additional step required.

Example 3.5

How much triple super phosphate (0-48-0) fertilizer would be needed to apply 2.5 lb P_2O_5/1,000 ft^2 to a 90,000 ft^2 driving range?

This fertilizer is 48% P_2O_5 by weight. In this case, the problem is worked in exactly the same way as the N problems.

First, determine how much 0-48-0 would be needed to obtain 2.5 lb P_2O_5.

1) $(X)(0.48) = 2.5$ lb P_2O_5

2) $X = \dfrac{2.5}{0.48}$

3) $X = 5.2$ lb 0 - 48 - 0

An application 5.2 lb of 0-48-0 fertilizer to 1,000 ft^2 will provide 2.5 lb P_2O_5.

Next, determine how much 0-48-0 will be needed to treat the 90,000-ft^2 driving range. Say the following words, "If 5.2 lb 0-48-0 are to be applied to 1,000 ft^2, how much will be needed to treat 90,000 ft^2?"

The problem is arranged as follows:

4) $\dfrac{5.2 \text{ lb}}{1,000 \text{ ft}^2} = \dfrac{X \text{ lb}}{90,000 \text{ ft}^2}$

5) $(X)(1,000) = (5.2)(90,000)$

6) $X = \dfrac{468,000}{1,000}$

7) $X = 468$ lb of 0 - 48 - 0 will be needed to treat the driving range

There will be other situations where application rates will be made on the basis of the individual elements, i.e., elemental P and K rather than P_2O_5 or K_2O.

Example 3.6

How much 0-0-50 (potassium sulfate) will be needed to apply 1 lb of K per 1,000 ft^2 to 90,000 ft^2 of greens?

Notice that the problem calls for K and not K_2O. This is an important difference, and large errors can occur if this fact is not taken into account.

To solve this problem, the same logic is required as that used in the N problems worked earlier, but there will be an additional step.

The first step is to determine how much K_2O will be required to achieve a rate of 1 lb K/1,000 ft^2. Remember that K_2O contains 83% K by weight. Some unknown quantity (X) of K_2O will be required to provide this 1 lb K.

1) $(X)(0.83) = 1$ lb K

2) $X = \dfrac{1}{0.83}$

3) $X = 1.2$ lb K_2O

It has been calculated that 1.2 lb of K_2O must be applied to each 1,000 ft^2 of green to achieve a rate of 1 lb K. The problem is now exactly like the N problems. The 0-0-50 fertilizer contains 50% K_2O by weight. It already has been calculated that 1.2 lb K_2O are required. Some unknown quantity (X) of 0-0-50 will be required to achieve the 1.2 lb of K_2O, therefore:

4) $(X)(0.50) = 1.2$ lb K_2O

5) $X = \dfrac{1.2}{0.50}$

6) $X = 2.4$ lb 0-0-50

If 2.4 lb of 0-0-50 are applied to 1,000 ft^2 of green, an application rate of 1.2 lb K_2O, or 1 lb K, will have been achieved.

If 2.4 lb of 0-0-50 are to be applied to 1,000 ft^2, how much would be needed to treat 90,000 ft^2?

1) $\dfrac{2.4}{1,000} = \dfrac{X}{90,000}$

2) $(1,000)(X) = (2.4)(90,000)$

3) $(1,000)(X) = 216,000$

4) $X = \dfrac{216,000}{1,000}$

5) $X = 216$

A total of 216 lb of 0-0-50 fertilizer will be needed to treat 90,000 ft^2 of greens at a rate of 1 lb K per 100 ft^2.

NOTICE!

There is a shortcut that can be used once the principles involved in this type of calculation are understood. Simply multiply the analysis, in this case 0.50, times the % K in K$_2$O (0.83) and divide the product into the amount of K that is desired (1 lb).

1) $(0.50)(0.83) = 0.415$

2) $\dfrac{1}{0.415} = 2.4$

Again, it has been calculated that 2.4 lb of 0-0-50 will be required to apply 1 lb of K. Use this shortcut only after the longer method is understood.

Problem 3.5

A starter fertilizer (13-25-6) is to be applied to 18 newly seeded tees. A total of 2 lb P is to be applied per 1,000 ft². The tees average 5,000 ft² each. How much 13-25-6 will be needed?

Problem 3.6

The recommendation is that 3 lb of K_2O per 1,000 ft² be applied to 50 acres of fairways. How much potassium sulfate (0-0-50) will be needed to make the application?

Problem 3.7

There are 160,000 ft^2 of greens on the course. A total of 4 lb N/1,000 ft^2 is to be applied during the season using a 20-2-10 fertilizer. The soil test indicates that 3 total lb of K should be applied/1,000 ft^2/yr.

How much additional potassium sulfate (0-0-50) will be needed to achieve the 3 lb K level?

CALCULATIONS INVOLVING LIQUID FERTILIZERS

The use of liquid fertilizers is becoming more common on golf courses. The principles involved in solving fertilizer problems that include liquid materials are similar to those used in solving problems for granular fertilizers, but the superintendent should recognize some distinctive features of these problems.

Example 3.7

A 12-4-4 liquid fertilizer is to be applied to greens at a rate sufficient to deliver 0.2 lb N per 1,000 ft². The fertilizer will be mixed with additional water and is to be applied in a total solution volume (fertilizer + water) of 2 gal per 1,000 ft². There is a total of 110,000 ft² of greens.

How much 12-4-4 will be needed for the application? If the spray tank to be used holds 100 gal, how much fertilizer and how much water should be placed in the tank when it is filled? How many 1,000 ft² will a 100-gal tank load treat? How many total tanks will have to be mixed to treat all of the greens?

A) How much 12-4-4 will be needed for the application?

The analysis has the same meaning with liquids as it does with granular fertilizers. It is the % by weight of N-P_2O_5-K_2O. However, in this case it is the weight of a liquid. Liquids are generally measured in gallons and not pounds. Fortunately, the number of lb N/gal is generally listed on the label of liquid fertilizers. If this information is not available, a gallon should be weighed and the amount of N calculated.

For example, if 1 gal of 12-4-4 weighs 10 lb, there would be:

$$(10)(0.12) = 1.2 \text{ lb N/gal}$$

For solving Section A, it will be assumed that the 12-4-4 contains 1.2 lb N/gal. To solve this problem, use the following logic: "If 1 gal contains 1.2 lb N, how many gal (X) contain 0.2 lb N?"

1) $\dfrac{1 \text{ gal}}{1.2 \text{ lb N}} = \dfrac{X \text{ gal}}{0.2 \text{ lb N}}$

2) X = 0.2 / 1.2

3) X = 0.17 gal

It has been calculated that 0.17 gal of fertilizer applied to 1,000 ft² of green will provide 0.2 lb N. The next logical question is, "If 0.17 gal is to be applied to 1,000 ft², how much (X) will be needed to treat 110,000 ft²?"

1) $\dfrac{0.17 \text{ gal}}{1,000 \text{ ft}^2} = \dfrac{\text{X gal}}{110,000 \text{ ft}^2}$

2) X = [(0.17)(110,000)] / 1,000

3) X = 18.7 gal

It has now been determined that 18.7 gal of 12-4-4 will be needed to treat the entire 110,000 ft² of greens at a rate of 0.2 lb N per 1,000 ft².

B) If the spray tank holds 100 gal, how much fertilizer and how much water should be placed in the tank when it is filled?

It is known that 2 gal total of solution are to be applied to every 1,000 ft². Of that 2 gal, 0.17 gal must be 12-4-4 liquid fertilizer; therefore, "If there is 0.17 gal of fertilizer in every 2 gal of solution, how much fertilizer (X) should there be in 100 gal of solution?"

1) $\dfrac{0.17}{2} = \dfrac{X}{100}$

2) X = $\dfrac{(0.17)(100)}{2}$

3) X = $\dfrac{17}{2}$

4) X = 8.5 gal of 12-4-4

For every 100-gal tank of spray that is mixed, 8.5 gal of 12-4-4 should be placed in the tank. It should then be filled with water to the 100-gal mark.

C) How many 1,000 ft² will a 100-gal tank of fertilizer solution treat?

Every 1,000 ft² will receive 2 gal solution. There are 100 gal of solution. Therefore, "If 1,000 ft² will be treated with 2 gal of solution, how many 1,000 ft² can be treated by 100 gal of solution?"

1) $\dfrac{1,000 \text{ ft}^2}{2 \text{ gal}} = \dfrac{X}{100 \text{ gal}}$

2) $X = \dfrac{(1,000)(100)}{2}$

3) $X = 50,000 \text{ ft}^2$

A total of 50,000 ft^2 can be treated at 0.2 lb N/1,000 ft^2 with a 100-gal tank of the mixture described in this problem.

D) How many tanks will be needed to treat the entire 110,000 ft^2?
If one tank treats 50,000 ft^2, how many tanks will be needed to treat 110,000 ft^2?

1) $\dfrac{1 \text{ tank}}{50,000 \text{ ft}^2} = \dfrac{X}{110,000 \text{ ft}^2}$

2) $X = \dfrac{110,000}{50,000}$

3) $X = 2.2$ tanks, or 220 total gal of solution

Problem 3.8

An 18-2-3 liquid fertilizer contains 1.8 lb N/gal, 0.09 lb P, and 0.25 lb K.

a. How many gallons of this fertilizer will be needed to apply 1 lb N per 1,000 ft^2 to 60,000 ft^2 of tees?

b. How much P and K was applied/1,000 ft^2?

Problem 3.9

A 200-gal sprayer is calibrated to release 3 gal total solution/1,000 ft^2. The goal is to apply 0.5 lb N/1,000 ft^2 to 25 ac of fairways using a 16-2-3 liquid fertilizer that contains 1.54 lb N/gal.

a. How many gal of 16-2-3 will be needed?

b. How much water and how much liquid fertilizer will be placed in each 200-gal tank?

MAKING ECONOMIC DECISIONS

An important part of golf course management is to use every budgeted dollar as efficiently as possible. To do this requires an understanding of fertilizer calculations and the use of that knowledge to determine which products deliver the greatest value for the lowest price.

Example 3.8

Of the following three fertilizers, which will be the best buy? Assume that N source and other variables are equal among the materials.

Fertilizer 1	Fertilizer 2	Fertilizer 3
10-3-5	20-6-10	12-4-4 (Liq. 1.2 lb N/gal)
$130/ton	$220/ton	$50/55 gal

N is the material that is usually of greatest interest. It is the cost per lb N that provides the best means of comparison among materials, not the cost per unit weight of fertilizer.

When working problems of this type, think cost/lb N and begin by placing a dollar sign ($) over the lb N:

This will prevent the common error of calculating the lb N/$.

$$\frac{\$}{\text{lb N}}$$

Next, calculate the amount of N in each of the fertilizers to be compared. Fertilizer 1 contains 10% N and the price is based on a ton:

$$(2,000 \text{ lb})(0.10) = 200 \text{ lb N}$$

Fertilizer 2 contains 20% N, and again the price is based on a ton:

$$(2,000 \text{ lb})(0.20) = 400 \text{ lb N}$$

Fertilizer 3 has 1.2 lb N/gal, and the price is based on a 55-gal barrel:

$$(55 \text{ gal})(1.2 \text{ lb N/gal}) = 66 \text{ lb N}$$

Next, divide the cost of the fertilizer by the number of lb N to determine the cost/lb N.

Fertilizer 1

$$\frac{\$130}{200 \text{ lb N}} = \$0.65 \text{ / lb N}$$

Fertilizer 2

$$\frac{\$220}{400 \text{ lb N}} = \$0.55 \text{ / lb N}$$

Fertilizer 3

$$\frac{\$50}{66 \text{ lb N}} = \$0.76 \text{ / lb N}$$

In this example, Fertilizer 2 at $0.55/lb N would be the least expensive and would be the best buy if all other factors were equal. It is important to remember that all other factors are rarely equal. Water-insoluble N sources will be more expensive than water-soluble sources and in many situations will be worth the extra cost. The amounts of P and K, although usually of less significance than N, should also be considered if the quantities differ significantly among the materials being compared. Cost per lb N, however, remains an important consideration in the decision-making process and should always be calculated when comparing fertilizers.

Problem 3.10

What is the cost/lb of N, P, and K for a ton (2,000 lb) of an 18-5-9 fertilizer that sells for $216/ton?

4

Pesticide Calculations

The pesticides used in the turf industry can be purchased in both dry and liquid forms. In both cases, the amount of active ingredient (a.i.) in the container is very important in the calculation process.

The application rate of materials is usually expressed as either a certain amount of a.i. per unit area (i.e., 1 lb a.i. per acre) or as a certain amount of product per unit area (i.e., 2 quarts per acre). The method by which the calculation is worked will vary with the way the rate is expressed, and the product label should be carefully read to gain a clear understanding of the desired rate and the nature of the product before the calculation is performed.

Dry pesticides can be purchased as Dusts (D), Granules (G), Wettable Powders (WP or W), Dry Flowables (DF), Dry Solubles (DS), Pellets (PS), Water-Dispersible Granules (WDG) and Soluble Powders (SP). These designations of formulation will be listed on the label with a number, i.e., 2.5G, 75WP, 50DF. These numbers represent the percentage by weight of the active ingredient (a.i.) in the material. A 2.5G material would be a granule with 2.5% active ingredient by weight. If the package weighed 100 lb, there would be 2.5 lb a.i. Likewise, a 75WP would be a Wettable Powder with 75% by weight a.i. and a 50DF would be a Dry Flowable with 50% a.i.

Liquid pesticides can be purchased as Emulsifiable Concentrates (EC or E), Solutions (S), Suspo-emulsions (SE), Liquids (L), Flowables (F), Micro Emulsions (ME) and Cation Liquids (CL), among other less common formulations. The EC formulation is the most widely used in the turfgrass industry. These designations of formulation are accompanied by numbers, i.e., 4EC or 3L. These numbers represent the number of lb a.i. per gal of the pesticide. The 4EC material would contain 4 lb a.i./gal and the 3L would contain 3 lb a.i./gal.

CALCULATIONS INVOLVING DRY PESTICIDES

The concept involved in solving this type of pesticide problem is exactly the same as that used in solving the fertilizer problems.
(See Chapter 3, Fertilizer Calculations.)

Example 4.1

A 2.5G preemergence herbicide is to be applied at a rate of 2 lb a.i./ac to 90,000 ft^2 of tees. How much of the material will be needed?

In this problem, 2 lb a.i./ac are needed. The herbicide is not pure a.i., however, but only 2.5% by weight a.i. Therefore, much more than 2 lb of product will need to be applied to each acre. The question is, how much more?

Drawing a picture similar to that used in the fertilizer calculations will be useful, and the mathematics involved will be the same.

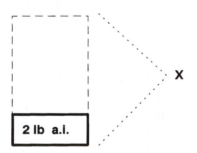

1) (X)(0.025) = 2 lb a.i.

2) X = 2/0.025

3) X = 80 lb of 2.5G/ac will be needed to apply 2 lb a.i./ac

The total area to be treated is 90,000 ft^2. One acre has 43,560 ft^2. Again, the problem is the same as the fertilizer problems.

Begin by asking the following question: "If 80 lb of preemergence herbicide are needed to treat 43,560 ft^2, how much (X) is needed to treat 90,000 ft^2?"

4) $\dfrac{80 \text{ lb}}{43{,}560 \text{ ft}^2} = \dfrac{X \text{ lb}}{90{,}000 \text{ ft}^2}$

5) $(43{,}560)\,(X) = (80)\,(90{,}000)$

6) $X = \dfrac{7{,}200{,}000}{43{,}560}$

7) $X = 165.3$ lb of the herbicide are needed to treat $90{,}000 \text{ ft}^2$ of tees.

Problem 4.1

A 10G insecticide is to be applied at 2 lb a.i./ac to 120,000 ft^2 of greens. How much of the insecticide will be needed?

Example 4.2

The label of a 50WDG insecticide recommends a rate of 1.5 lb a.i./ac. How much of this material in ounces (16 oz/lb) would be needed to treat an 8,700 ft^2 green?

Fifty percent of some amount (X) of this material is needed to obtain the 1.5 lb a.i. that would be required to treat an acre. Arrange the problem as follows:

1) $(X)(0.50) = 1.5$ lb a.i.

2) $X = \dfrac{1.5}{0.50}$

3) $X = 3$ lb

If 3 lb of this product are applied to 1 ac, 1.5 lb of a.i. will have been applied.

Next, calculate how much of the product would be needed to treat the 8,700 ft^2 green. It may help to say to yourself, "If 3 lb are needed to treat 43,560 ft^2 (1 ac), how much would be needed to treat 8,700 ft^2?" Set up a proportion and solve the problem by cross-multiplying and dividing.

4) $\dfrac{3 \text{ lb}}{43{,}560 \text{ ft}^2} = \dfrac{X \text{ lb}}{8{,}700 \text{ ft}^2}$

5) $(43{,}560)(X) = (3)(8{,}700)$

6) $X = \dfrac{26{,}100}{43{,}560}$

7) $X = 0.60$ lb

An application of 0.60 lb of product to 8,700 ft^2 will be equivalent to a rate of 1.5 lb/ac.

Next, convert to ounces of product.

If there are 16 oz/lb, how many ounces are in 0.60 lb?

8) $\dfrac{16 \text{ oz}}{1 \text{ lb}} = \dfrac{X \text{ oz}}{0.60 \text{ lb}}$

9) $X = (16)(0.60)$

10) X = 9.6 oz

Exactly 9.6 oz of this product should be applied to the 8,700-ft^2 green.

A shortcut to convert the pounds to ounces would be to simply multiply the 16 oz times 0.60. The answer, 9.6 oz, is the same. Setting the problems up in proportions, though, will help you keep your thought process ordered as you go through multiple-step problems.

Problem 4.2

A 75WP herbicide is to be applied at a rate of 10 lb a.i./ac to 40 ac of fairways. How much of this material must be purchased for the application?

Problem 4.3

A 50DF insecticide is to be applied at a rate of 1.8 lb a.i./ac. How much is needed to treat five tees that total 60,000 ft^2?

Problem 4.4

A 90DF fungicide is to be applied at 6 lb product/ac.

a) How much would be needed to treat 35,000 ft^2 of turf?

b) How much a.i. was applied per acre?

c) How much total a.i. was applied to 35,000 ft^2?

Example 4.3

A 75WP herbicide is to be applied at a rate of 14 lb product per acre to 20,000 ft^2 of fairway. How much of the herbicide is needed?

In this problem, the formulation and % a.i. are not involved in the calculation. It simply calls for a certain amount of product per unit area.

If 14 lb of product are to be applied to 1 ac, how many lb (X) will be needed to treat 20,000 ft^2? (1 ac = 43,560 ft^2.)

1) $\dfrac{14 \text{ lb}}{43,560 \text{ ft}^2} = \dfrac{X \text{ lb}}{20,000 \text{ ft}^2}$

2) $(43,560)(X) = (14)(20,000)$

3) $X = \dfrac{280,000}{43,560}$

4) $X = 6.4$ lb of product will be required to treat 20,000 ft^2.

Pesticide reporting forms in many states require the reporting of application rates in lb a.i./ac, lb a.i./1,000 ft^2, and total amount of a.i. applied per application.

Next, calculate how many lb a.i. were applied/1,000 ft^2, per ac, and how many lb a.i. were applied to the 20,000 ft^2.

There were 14 lb of product applied per acre. The product is 75% a.i. Therefore:

5) $(14)(0.75) = 10.5$ lb a.i.

This is equivalent to a rate of 10.5 lbs a.i./acre.

If 10.5 lb a.i. were applied per acre (43,560 ft^2), how many lb a.i. were applied per 1,000 ft^2?

6) $\dfrac{10.5 \text{ lb a.i.}}{43,560 \text{ ft}^2} = \dfrac{X \text{ lb a.i.}}{1,000 \text{ ft}^2}$

7) $(43,560)(X) = (10.5)(1,000)$

8) $X = 0.24$ lb a.i./1,000 ft^2

Finally, if 6.4 lb product were applied to 20,000 ft^2, how much total a.i. was applied?

9) $(6.4)(0.75) = 4.8$ lb a.i.

A total of 4.8 lb a.i. was applied to the 20,000 ft^2 of fairways.

CALCULATIONS OF COST PER POUND ACTIVE INGREDIENT

Calculations of the cost of material per pound a.i. for the dry chemicals can be useful in choosing the least expensive formulation.

In situations where the recommended rate is made on the basis of pounds of product per unit area, and not on the basis of pounds a.i. per unit area, the calculations are much easier. But care must be taken that the problem is clearly understood to avoid serious errors in application rate.

Example 4.4

There are two granular formulations of the same pesticide. One is a 2G and the other is a 5G. The carrier for the two materials and the recommended rate of a.i. per acre are the same. A 50-lb bag of the 2G sells for $35.00 and a 50-lb bag of the 5G sells for $65.00. Which is the best buy?

In solving this type of problem, think dollars per lb of a.i. It will help to write that down first to prevent errors.

$$\frac{\$}{\text{lb a.i.}}$$

Next, calculate the number of lb of a.i. in each bag.

2G: $(50 \text{ lb})(0.02) = 1$ lb a.i.

5G: $(50 \text{ lb})(0.05) = 2.5$ lb a.i.

Then calculate the cost per lb a.i.

2G: $35/1 lb a.i. = $35 per lb a.i.

5G: $65/2.5 lb a.i. = $26 per lb a.i.

The 2G at first appears to be the best buy because it sells for a lower unit price per 50-lb bag. However, calculating the cost per lb a.i. clearly shows that the 5G is the best buy.

Problem 4.5

A 60WDG preemergence herbicide sells for $98.00 for a 10-lb bag. The same active ingredient in a 5G sells for $42.00 for a 50-lb bag. Which is the most expensive?

CALCULATIONS INVOLVING LIQUID PESTICIDES

This type of problem is considerably different from the problem worked with dry materials, although the logic and mathematics used to solve them will be similar.

Example 4.5

A 4EC material is to be applied at a rate of 1.5 lb a.i. per acre to a 6,000 ft^2 green. How much material in fluid ounces will be needed to treat the green?

- 1 ac = 43,560 ft^2
- 1 gal = 128 fl oz

The designation of 4EC indicates that this is an emulsifiable concentrate that contains 4 lb a.i./gal. The recommended rate is 1.5 lb a.i./ac. A logical place to start in solving this problem would be to determine how many gallons would be needed to deliver the 1.5 lb a.i.

Begin with the following question and calculation: "If 1 gal contains 4 lb a.i., how many gallons (X) will be needed to apply 1.5 lb a.i.?"

1) $\dfrac{1 \text{ gal}}{4 \text{ lb a.i.}} = \dfrac{X}{1.5 \text{ lb a.i.}}$

2) $X = \dfrac{1.5}{4}$

3) $X = 0.375$ gal

The calculation shows that 0.375 gal of this material contains 1.5 lb a.i., the amount needed to treat 1 ac.

There are 128 fl oz in each gal; how many (X) fl oz are in 0.375 gal?

4) $\dfrac{128 \text{ fl oz}}{1 \text{ gal}} = \dfrac{X \text{ fl oz}}{0.375 \text{ gal}}$

5) $X = (128)(0.375)$

6) $X = 48$ fl oz will treat 1 ac with 1.5 lb a.i.

The area to be treated is 6,000 ft^2. The next question to be asked is, "If 48 fl oz are required to treat 1 ac (43,560 ft^2), how much would be needed to treat 6,000 ft^2?"

7) $\dfrac{48 \text{ fl oz}}{43,560} = \dfrac{X \text{ fl oz}}{6,000}$

8) (43,560)(X) = (48)(6,000)

9) X = $\dfrac{288,000}{43,560}$

10) X = 6.6 fl oz will treat 6000 ft^2 at a rate equivalent to 1.5 lb a.i./ac.

Problem 4.6

A 3L herbicide is to be applied at 2 lb a.i./ac. How many ounces will be needed to treat 25,000 ft^2 of tees? (1 gal contains 128 oz.)

As was the case with the dry pesticides, recommendations will sometimes specify a certain amount of liquid pesticide per unit area. Again, be sure that the recommendation is clearly understood before these calculations are performed.

Example 4.6

The label of a 2EC insecticide indicates that 2 fl oz of product should be applied per 1,000 ft^2. How much will be needed to treat 110,000 ft^2 of greens? (There are 128 fl oz per gal.)

The fact that this is a 2EC product does not enter into the calculation. The label simply states that 2 fl oz of product are needed per 1,000 ft^2.

1) $\dfrac{2 \text{ fl oz}}{1,000 \text{ ft}^2} = \dfrac{X \text{ fl oz}}{110,000 \text{ ft}^2}$

2) $(1,000)(X) = (2)(110,000)$

3) $X = \dfrac{220,000}{1,000}$

4) $X = 220 \text{ fl oz}$

5) $\dfrac{220}{128} = 1.7 \text{ gal are required to treat } 110,000 \text{ ft}^2.$

How many lb a.i. were applied per 1,000 ft^2 at this rate?
A 2EC contains 2 lb a.i./gal, and there are 128 oz in a gal.

6) $\dfrac{2 \text{ lb}}{128 \text{ oz}} = \dfrac{X \text{ lb}}{2 \text{ oz}}$

7) $128X = (2)(2)$

8) $X = \dfrac{4}{128}$

9) $X = 0.03 \text{ lb a.i./1,000 ft}^2$

How much a.i. was applied to the 110,000 ft^2 of greens?
There are 2 lb a.i. in 1 gal. How much is there in 1.7 gal?

10) $\dfrac{2 \text{ lb}}{1 \text{ gal}} = \dfrac{X}{1.7 \text{ gal}}$

11) $X = (2)(1.7)$

12) $X = 3.4 \text{ lb a.i. were applied}$

Problem 4.7

A 4F fungicide is to be applied at 12 lb a.i./ac.

a) How much material in fluid ounces will be needed to treat a 9,000-ft^2 green?

b) How much material in a.i. was applied per acre?

c) How much a.i. was applied to the 9,000 ft^2?

Example 4.7

The same insecticide is available as a 4EC, a 50WP, and a 5G. The 4EC sells for $28/gal, the 50WP sells for $150 for a 50-lb bag, and a 50-lb bag of the 5G sells for $25. Which formulation costs the least per lb a.i.?

Begin by determining how many lb a.i. are in each container:

4EC: There are 4 lb a.i./gal. At a cost of $28/gal,

$$\$28/4 \text{ lb a.i.} = \$7/\text{lb a.i.}$$

50WP: The material is 50% a.i. At a cost of $150 for 50 lb,

$$(50 \text{ lb})(0.5) = 25 \text{ lb a.i.}$$

$$\$150/25 \text{ lb a.i.} = \$6/\text{lb a.i.}$$

5G: The material is 5% a.i. At a cost of $25 for 50 lb,

$$(50 \text{ lb})(0.05) = 2.5 \text{ lb a.i.}$$

$$\$25/2.5 \text{ lb a.i.} = \$10/\text{lb a.i.}$$

The 50WP product at $6/lb a.i. is the least expensive material.

Problem 4.8

A fungicide is available in a 4.5F for $150.00/gal, a 50WDG for $123.00 for a 4-lb bag, and a 1.5G for $45.10 for a 35-lb bag. What is the cost per pound a.i. for each material?

Spreader and Sprayer Calibration

In this chapter, the mathematics involved in the calibration of spreaders and spray equipment will be presented. Practical tips for the mechanics of calibration in the field are included, along with several examples and sample problems. If you are not familiar with the mathematics involved in fertilizer and pesticide calculations, review Chapters 3 and 4 first.

SPREADER CALIBRATION

There are several types of spreaders for the application of dry fertilizers and pesticides (Figure 5.1). The principles involved in their calibration are basically the same, although the mechanics of performing the calibration process will vary among the different types of equipment.

Drop Spreaders

We will begin with the basic "drop spreader." These spreaders are used for applying dry fertilizers and pesticides to turf. They can also be useful for applying seed during the establishment process. Product or seed is placed in the hopper of the spreader. A lever is operated to turn the flow off and on, and material is released from the bottom of the hopper. The flow rate can be adjusted with a set mechanism to allow varying amounts of material to be released. These set mechanisms will have either letters or numbers (Figure 5.2). The higher the letter or number, the more material is released. The goal of calibration is to set the flow-control mechanism to release the desired amount of material per unit area. *Always record the setting for future use once it's been determined for a given material.*

Some spreaders come with instructions that provide clues to the desired setting for given products. These settings should always be checked. Product particle sizes vary, and rarely will the suggested setting provide

Figure 5.1. Drop-spreader on left and rotary spreader on right.

Figure 5.2. Set mechanisms for various drop-type and rotary spreaders.

exactly the rate that is listed in the manual. Once the rate has been determined for a given material, it should be checked each time new product is
purchased to be sure that the setting is proper.

The process of calibration begins by calculating how much material should be released on a given area when the spreader is properly set. From that point on, it is a trial and error process. A test setting is selected. The spreader is operated over a premeasured strip and the material released from the spreader is retrieved and weighed. The setting is adjusted until the proper release rate is achieved.

An effective way to continuously check the calibration as the application is made on larger areas is to determine how many bags of material are needed to make the entire application. For instance, if eight bags are going to be needed to make the treatment and only two bags have been used when half the area has been treated, something's wrong. Experienced applicators conduct continuous mental checks of this type as the application proceeds.

There are several methods of retrieving the released material. It can simply be swept up with a broom and dustpan from a clean floor. The spreader can be operated over a plastic sheet or canvas, which results in easier retrieval and less chance for error. Catch trays can also be made to fit on the bottom of the spreader to collect the released material (Figure 5.3). If a larger scale is available, the entire spreader can be weighed before and after the application, or a known weight of material can be placed in the hopper and can be reweighed following application to a test strip.

The goal in applying any material to turf is to apply it as uniformly as possible. A highly skilled applicator with the best equipment may be able to do this with a single pass over the turf. A single pass, however, gener-

Figure 5.3. Drop-spreader with catch tray.

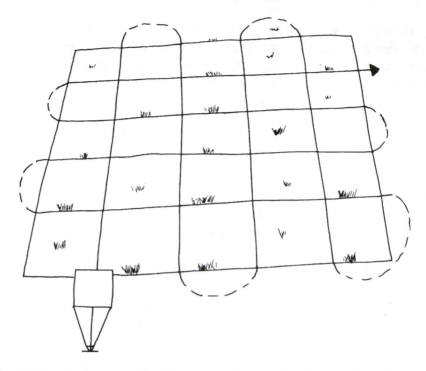

Figure 5.4. Apply one-half of the material in one direction and the other one-half at right angles to the first pass.

ally leads to skips and overlaps. The best way to uniformly apply material, whether it be liquid or dry, is to calibrate the equipment for half of the desired rate and to make two passes over the area. The second pass should be made at a right angle to the first (Figure 5.4). The calibrated rate of application will depend on whether one or two passes are to be made.

Example 5.1

A 42-in.-wide drop spreader is to be used to apply a 15-2-10 fertilizer to a green at a rate of 1 lb N/1,000 ft². The material is to be applied in two passes over the turf to assure uniformity. The spreader should be calibrated to apply 0.5 lb N/1,000 ft². There are 100,000 ft² of greens to be treated.

Step 1. Make sure that you have all of the equipment that will be needed for the calibration. In this case, the spreader will be operated over a plastic sheet. The test area will be 20 ft long, so the sheet should be at least 22 to 25 ft in length. You will also need a scale that will weigh accurately to the nearest 1/10 oz (or to the nearest gram if a metric scale is to be used). Perform the calibration in a clean, smooth surface, such as a cleanly swept shop floor. Tape the edges of the sheet to the floor and mark the 20-ft test strip.

Step 2. Calculate how much fertilizer should be released from the spreader when it is properly calibrated to release 0.5 lb N/1,000 ft^2.

$$(X)(0.15) = 0.5 \text{ lb N}$$

$$X = \frac{0.5}{0.15}$$

$$X = 3.33 \text{ lb fertilizer}$$

If 3.33 lb of 15-2-10 fertilizer are applied per 1,000 ft^2, the desired rate of 0.5 lb N/1,000 ft^2 will have been achieved.

The test strip over which the spreader will be operated is 20 ft long and the spreader is 42 in. wide.

20 ft

42 in.

Convert the width of the spreader from inches to feet. This can be done by setting up a proportion, followed by cross-multiplying and dividing.

If 1 ft has 12 in., how many feet are there in 42 in.?

$$\frac{1 \text{ ft}}{12 \text{ in.}} = \frac{X \text{ ft}}{42 \text{ in.}}$$

$$(X)(12) = (1)(42)$$

$$X = \frac{42}{12}$$

$$X = 3.5 \text{ ft}$$

If the mathematics in the above step are thoroughly understood, a short-cut can be used to convert inches to feet. Simply divide the 42 in. by 12:

$$\frac{42}{12} = 3.5 \text{ ft}$$

The test area is 3.5 ft by 20 ft, or

$$(3.5 \text{ ft})(20 \text{ ft}) = 70 \text{ ft}^2$$

If 3.33 lb of 15-2-10 fertilizer are to be applied to 1,000 ft^2 to achieve a rate of 0.5 lb N/1,000 ft^2, how much should be released by the spreader on a 70-ft^2 test area when it is properly set?

$$\frac{3.33 \text{ lb}}{1,000 \text{ ft}^2} = \frac{X \text{ lb}}{70 \text{ ft}^2}$$

$$(X)(1,000) = (3.33)(70)$$

$$X = \frac{233.1}{1,000}$$

$$X = 0.2331 \text{ lb}$$

One lb contains 16 oz, which is:

$$(16)(0.2331) = 3.7 \text{ oz of 15-2-10 fertilizer}$$

When the spreader is properly set, 3.7 oz of fertilizer will be collected from the 70-ft^2 test area.

If you are working with the metric scale, figure that there are 454 g in one lb. In this case, $454 \times 0.2331 = 106$ g should be released on the test area.

Step 3. Spread the plastic sheet on a smooth surface and mark off 20 ft. Next, choose a test setting on your spreader. As you gain experience, esti-mating the setting will be easier, but for the initial setting on a new spreader or with a new material, you may have to guess at the setting. Operate the spreader over the 20-ft test area. Approach the test area at the uniform walking speed that will be used consistently during the application process. The flow rate will remain constant, and walking speed will have a major effect on application rate. Be sure to start the flow of material at the beginning of the test area and stop it exactly at the end of the 20-ft strip.

Collect the material from the plastic sheet and weigh it. If it weighs less that 3.7 oz you will need to increase the setting, and if it is more than 3.7 oz you will need to decrease the setting. You will soon learn that small changes in the setting result in large changes in flow rate. A doubling of the setting number will not result in a doubling of flow rate; the increase will likely be more in the range of 10-fold with a doubling in the setting.

It may take from five to ten tries to accurately set the spreader with a new material.

As a final check to any calibration procedure, calculations should be made during the application process to be sure that the right amount of material is being delivered. In the above example, 3.33 lb of fertilizer should be applied per 1,000 ft^2 per pass. There will be two passes. If the first green treated measures 8,000 ft^2, how much fertilizer will be needed to treat it?

The 3.33 lb/1,000 ft^2 is equivalent to 0.5 lb N/1,000 ft^2. This application is to be made in two directions for a total of 6.66 lb of fertilizer per 1,000 ft^2.

If 6.66 lb of fertilizer are to be applied to 1,000 ft^2, how much is needed to treat an 8,000-ft^2 green?

$$\frac{6.66 \text{ lb}}{1,000 \text{ ft}^2} = \frac{X \text{ lb}}{8,000 \text{ ft}^2}$$

$$(1,000)(X) = (6.66)(8,000)$$

$$X = \frac{53,280}{1,000}$$

$$X = 53.3 \text{ lb of fertilizer}$$

Slightly more than a 50-lb bag should applied to the 8,000 ft^2 green when the spreader is properly calibrated. If it is obvious after the first green is treated that significantly more or less than this amount has been applied, the calibration should be rechecked.

When the entire application has been completed, double check to be sure that the amount of product required to complete the application has been applied. In this example, the area to be treated is 100,000 ft^2. If each 1,000 ft^2 is to receive 6.66 lb of 15-2-10, then how much will be needed to treat 100,000 ft^2?

$$\frac{6.66 \text{ lb}}{1,000 \text{ ft}^2} = \frac{X \text{ lb}}{100,000 \text{ ft}^2}$$

$$(1,000)(X) = (6.66)(100,000)$$

$$X = \frac{666,000}{1,000}$$

$$X = 666 \text{ lb of } 15\text{-}2\text{-}10$$

A total of 666 lb of the 15-2-10 fertilizer will be applied to the 100,000 ft^2 of greens.

If the fertilizer is in 50-lb bags,

$$\frac{666}{50} = 13.3 \text{ bags}$$

A little more than 13 bags (13.3) will be used if the application is properly made.

Problem 5.1

A 54-in.-wide drop spreader is to be calibrated to apply 1 lb N/1,000 ft^2 using a 10-3-6 fertilizer in a single pass. A 25-ft test strip will be used for the calibration. A catch tray will be attached to the bottom of the spreader. How many ounces of 10-3-6 fertilizer will there be in the tray when the spreader is properly calibrated?

The spreader will be used to treat 130,000 ft^2 of tees. How many 50-lb bags will be needed to make the application?

Example 5.2

A 2G preemergence herbicide is to be applied to the tees at a rate of 2.5 lb a.i./ac with a 36-in.-wide drop spreader. The spreader is to be calibrated on a plastic sheet with a 30-ft test strip. The treatment will be made with a single pass, and it will be calibrated to release the full rate. How many ounces of the 2G herbicide will be released on the 30-ft strip when the spreader is properly calibrated? The material comes in 40-lb bags.

The area to be treated measures 65,000 ft². How many 40-lb bags will be needed to make the application?

Step 1. Determine how much product will be needed per acre to deliver 2.5 lb a.i./ac?

$$(X)(0.02) = 2.5 \text{ lb a.i.}$$

$$X = \frac{2.5}{0.02}$$

$$X = 125 \text{ lb herbicide}$$

An application of 125 lb of the herbicide to 1 ac is required to apply 2.5 lb a.i.

Step 2. Determine how much material would be applied to a 30-ft test strip.

The spreader is 36 in. wide. Convert inches to feet by dividing by 12 inches.

$$\frac{36 \text{ in.}}{12 \text{ in.}} = 3 \text{ ft wide}$$

The spreader is 3 ft wide and the test strip is 30 ft long. The test area is

$$(3 \text{ ft})(30 \text{ ft}) = 90 \text{ ft}^2$$

How much of the herbicide should be applied to a 90-ft² test area? An acre is 43,560. If 125 lb are needed to cover 43,560 ft², how much would be needed to treat 90 ft²?

$$\frac{125 \text{ lb}}{43,560 \text{ ft}^2} = \frac{X \text{ lb}}{90 \text{ ft}^2}$$

$$(X)(43,560) = (125)(90)$$

$$X = \frac{11,250}{43,560}$$

$$X = 0.258 \text{ lb of herbicide}$$

There are 16 oz/lb. Therefore:

$$(16)(0.258) = 4.1 \text{ oz}$$

There will be 4.1 oz of the herbicide applied to the test area when the fertilizer spreader is properly calibrated.

If the herbicide comes in 40-lb bags, how many bags should be used for the application?

If 125 lb of herbicide are to be applied to an acre ($43,560 \text{ ft}^2$), how much will be needed to treat $65,000 \text{ ft}^2$?

$$\frac{125 \text{ lb}}{43,560 \text{ ft}^2} = \frac{X \text{ lb}}{65,000 \text{ ft}^2}$$

$$(43,560)(X) = (125)(65,000)$$

$$X = \frac{8,125,000}{43,560}$$

$$X = 186.5 \text{ lb}$$

There are 40 lb/bag:

$$\frac{186.6}{40} = 4.7 \text{ bags}$$

A little less than 5 bags (4.7) will have been applied to the $65,000 \text{ ft}^2$ if the spreader is properly calibrated.

Problem 5.2

A 5G insecticide is to be applied to the greens at a rate of 3.0 lb a.i./ ac. A 48-in.-wide spreader will be used for the treatment. A 50-ft test strip will be used and the material will be collected on a plastic sheet. The spreader will be calibrated at 1.5 lb a.i./ac, and two passes will be used to make the 1.5-lb a.i./ac treatment. How much material will be released from this spreader on the test strip when the spreader is properly calibrated?

There are 150,000 ft^2 of greens to be treated. The insecticide comes in 42-lb bags. How many bags will have been used if the treatment is properly made?

Rotary Spreaders

Rotary spreaders have a spinning disk located below the hopper that throws the fertilizer in a semicircular pattern ahead of the machine (Figure 5.5). These spreaders can cover large areas quickly, and are generally the preferred method of applying granular materials if large areas are to be treated. The rotary spreader requires more experience than the drop spreader for uniform application of material, but in the hands of an experienced operator very uniform applications can be achieved.

Rotary spreaders are also more difficult to properly calibrate than drop spreaders. The fan of material distributed by the spinning disk will vary in diameter with the particle size and density of the material being applied. Different makes and models of spreaders are also designed to be used with varying amounts of overlap. Read the instruction for the spreader before beginning the calibration process. There may by recommended settings included for certain types of fertilizers and granular pesticides. These settings should always be verified with calibration before any new spreader or new material is used on the course.

Rotary spreaders may be designed to spread from wheel track to wheel track (Figure 5.6). The Lesco spreader is an example of this type of spreader. They may also be designed to overlap slightly at the edge of the fan of material (Figure 5.7). The Scotts rotary spreaders are designed to be operated in this pattern. Both spreaders may be used to apply the desired amount of material in a single directional pass over the area. However, the greatest uniformity will be achieved by calibrating them to deliver half of the desired application rate and then by following the dual application pattern in Figure 5.4.

There may be other attachments and modifications on some models of spreaders. Those designed to overlap from wheel track to wheel track may have a moveable shield that can be used to direct the fan of material along fence lines and other areas where spreading material is not desired (Figure 5.8). The Scotts spreaders have a cone on the base of the spreader designed to provide even application from right to left. Be sure to read directions for the use of these attachments before calibrating the spreader.

Begin the calibration process by applying a test strip of the material to determine the effective swath width (the diameter of the distribution pattern). Again, this will vary with the material. It is usually in the range of 8 to 15 ft. Once the swath width is known, the calibration process becomes

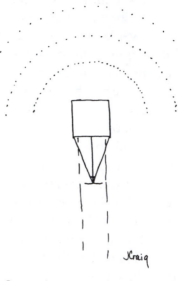

Figure 5.5. Spread pattern of rotary type spreader.

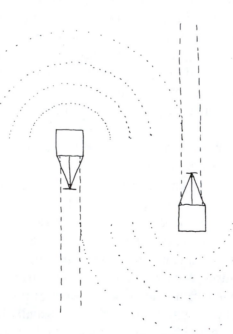

Figure 5.6. Overlapping wheel track to wheel track.

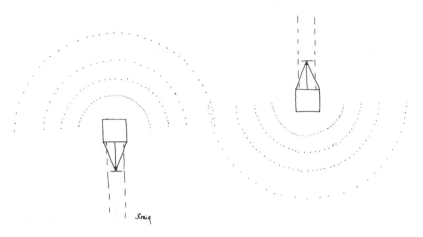

Figure 5.7. Overlapping slightly at the edge of the fan of material.

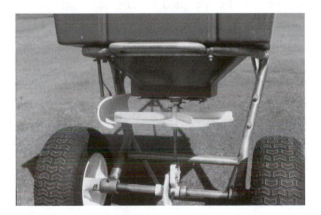

Figure 5.8. Shield to direct the flow of material.

the same as that used for drop spreaders, but the determination of the amount of the material applied to the test strip is more difficult.

As with drop spreaders, the process of determining the amount of product released from the spreader can be handled in a number of ways.

Method 1

The product can be applied to the test strip on a smooth surface and swept up with a broom, or it can be applied on a large plastic sheet. Because of the width of the test strip, this is often not practical. On a smooth surface, the materials tend to bounce and roll beyond the normal application area.

Method 2

A known amount of material can be placed in the hopper. The spreader can be operated over the test strip. The hopper can then be emptied and the remaining material weighed. The difference between the original weight and the post-application weight is the weight of material applied to the test strip. This is a time-consuming method, and it requires a lot of space to apply the test strips, but it is an accurate way of determining release rates. If a large enough scale is available, the entire spreader with the fertilizer in the hopper can be weighed before and after the treatment.

Method 3

A calibration catch tray for broadcast spreaders called the PennPro Collector® can be used to catch the material (Figure 5.9). An initial test strip will still be needed to measure effective swath width, but once that has been done this is a very effective way of calibrating broadcast spreaders.

As with the drop spreader, walking speed has a large impact on application rate, and a uniform walking speed must be used for both calibration and application.

Figure 5.9. Rotary spreader with Penn Pro Collector®.

Example 5.3

A rotary spreader is to be calibrated to apply 1 lb N/1,000 ft^2 in two passes. The fertilizer is a 20-2-15. The spreader has an effective spread width of 12 ft, and it is to be overlapped from wheel track to wheel track (Figure 5.6). A 60-ft test strip is to be used. How much fertilizer will be released from the spreader on the 60-ft test strip when it is properly calibrated? How many 50-lb bags of the 20-2-15 fertilizer will be needed to treat 3.5 acres of turf?

Step 1. The effective spread width is already known to be 12 ft. The length of the test strip is 60 ft. Therefore:

$$(12 \text{ ft})(60 \text{ ft}) = 720 \text{ ft}^2$$

Notice something special about this spreader. It is designed to spread from wheel track to wheel track. This means that in a single directional application, the area is covered twice. Therefore, the spreader must be calibrated at 1/4 the desired application rate. In this case, it should be calibrated to release 0.25 lb N/1,000 ft^2. Operating it in one direction, with the overlap, will result in 0.5 lb N/1,000 ft^2. When it is operated at right angles to the original direction, a total of 1 lb N/1,000 ft^2 will have been applied.

Step 2. Next, determine how much 20-2-15 fertilizer will be needed to apply 0.25 lb N/1,000 ft^2.

$$(X)(0.20) = 0.25$$

$$X = \frac{0.25}{0.20}$$

$$X = 1.25 \text{ lb } 20\text{-}2\text{-}15$$

If 1.25 lb 20-2-15 are applied to 1,000 ft^2, 0.25 lb N will have been applied.

Step 3. Now determine how much 20-2-15 fertilizer will be released on 720 ft^2, the area of the test strip.

If 1.25 lb are to be applied to 1,000 ft^2, how much will be applied to 720 ft^2?

$$\frac{1.25 \text{ lb}}{1,000 \text{ ft}^2} = \frac{X \text{ lb}}{720 \text{ ft}^2}$$

$$(1,000)(X) = (1.25)(720)$$

$$X = \frac{900}{1,000}$$

$$X = 0.9 \text{ lb of fertilizer}$$

Slightly less than 1 pound (0.9 lb) of fertilizer will be released on the 60-ft test strip when the spreader is properly calibrated. There are 16 oz/lb, therefore:

$$(16)(0.9) = 14.4 \text{ oz of fertilizer will be released on the strip}$$

Step 4. Weigh the fertilizer in the spreader (or the spreader and fertilizer together if a large scale is available).

Step 5. Select a test setting and operate the spreader over the selected area. Determine how much material was released by subtracting the original weight from the weight after application, and adjust the setting.

Step 6. Continue this process until the desired amount of 14.4 oz (0.9 lb) of material is consistently released.

Step 7. Check the setting on a larger test area. In this case, a nurse green or practice green would be suitable. Remember that 1.25 lb of 20-2-15 fertilizer will be released in a single pass. With the overlap to the wheel tracks and application in two directions, a total of $1.25 \times 4 = 5$ lb of 20-2-15 fertilizer would be applied to 1,000 ft^2.

A 10,000-ft^2 nurse green, for instance, would receive

$$\frac{5 \text{ lb}}{1,000 \text{ ft}^2} = \frac{X \text{ lb}}{10,000 \text{ ft}^2}$$

$$X = 50 \text{ lb } 20\text{-}2\text{-}15$$

If the spreader is properly calibrated, an application from wheel track to wheel track applied in both directions to a 10,000-ft^2 green should require 50 lb of 20-2-15.

If the application rate varies significantly from this amount, re-check the calibration.

Step 8. Finally, determine how many 50-lb bags will be needed to treat 3.5 ac.

There are 43,560 ft^2/ac. The 3.5 ac is equal to $3.5 \times 43,560 = 152,460$ ft^2. If 50 lb are required to treat 10,000 ft^2, then how many pounds are needed to treat 152,460 ft^2?

$$\frac{50 \text{ lb}}{10,000 \text{ ft}^2} = \frac{X \text{ lb}}{152,460 \text{ ft}^2}$$

$$(10,000)(X) = (50)(152,460)$$

$$X = \frac{7,623,000}{10,000}$$

$$X = 762.3 \text{ lb fertilizer}$$

There are 50 lb/bag:

$$\frac{762.3}{50} = 15.2 \text{ bags}$$

Slightly more than 15 bags (15.2) will be needed to treat the 3.5 ac of turf.

Problem 5.3

A rotary spreader that is designed to overlap from wheel track to wheel track is to be used to apply an 18-5-9 fertilizer to 160,000 ft^2 of tees. The rate of application is 0.75 lb N/1,000 ft^2. A test strip of 100 ft is to be used, and the effective spread width has been determined to be 15 ft.

If the material is in 33.3-lb bags, how many bags will be needed to make the treatment?

Example 5.4

A spreader designed to overlap slightly at the edge of the spread width (Figure 5.7) is to be calibrated to apply a granular fertilizer/fungicide combination at a rate of 1.4 lb a.i./ac. The material is a 23-3-5 fertilizer with 2.05% a.i. that comes in a 33.3-lb bag. A 100-ft test strip will be used for the calibration. The effective spread width with this material is 8 ft. The spreader is to be calibrated to deliver one-half of the recommended rate per pass. The treatment will be made in two passes at right angles to each other. If 120,000 ft^2 of greens are to be treated, how many bags of material would be required to treat the area?

How much N will be applied per 1,000 ft^2 at this application rate?

Step 1. Begin by calculating how much of this product is needed per acre. An application rate of 1.4 lb a.i. with a 2.05% a.i. product will require an application of:

$$(X)(0.0205) = 1.4 \text{ lb a.i.}$$

$$X = \frac{1.4}{0.0205}$$

$$X = 68.3 \text{ lb product}$$

If 68.3 lb of product are applied to 1 ac (43,560 ft^2), the recommended rate of 1.4 lb a.i. of the fungicide will have been achieved.

Step 2. Next, determine how much would be released on the 100-ft test strip when the spreader is properly calibrated. Remember that it is to be calibrated to release one-half of the recommended rate. Therefore:

$$\frac{68.3}{2} = 34.2 \text{ lb}$$

of product will be applied per acre per pass.

The test strip is 100 ft long and 8 ft wide, for a total of 100 ft × 8 ft = 800 ft^2.

If 34.2 lb of product is to be applied to 43,560 ft^2, how much would be applied to an 800-ft^2 test strip?

$$\frac{34.2 \text{ lb}}{43,560 \text{ ft}^2} = \frac{X \text{ lb}}{800 \text{ ft}^2}$$

$$(43,560)(X) = (34.2)(800)$$

$$X = \frac{27,360}{43,560}$$

$$X = 0.628 \text{ lb}$$

A total of 0.628 lb, or $16 \times 0.628 = 10$ oz, of material should be applied on the test strip when the spreader is properly calibrated.

Step 3. Continue to apply material over the test strip and adjust the setting until the proper rate has been achieved.

Step 4. If 68.3 lb of material is to be applied to 43,560 ft, how much will be needed for 120,000 ft^2?

$$\frac{68.3 \text{ lb}}{43,560 \text{ ft}^2} = \frac{X \text{ lb}}{120,000 \text{ ft}^2}$$

$$(43,560)(X) = (68.3)(120,000)$$

$$X = \frac{8,196,000}{43,560}$$

$$X = 188 \text{ lb}$$

A total of 188 lb of material, or $188/33.5 = 5.6$ bags of material, will be needed.

Problem 5.4

A rotary spreader is to be calibrated to deliver a 2G insecticide at a rate of 4 lb a.i./ac to 140,000 ft^2 of tees. The effective spread width is 11 ft. It will be calibrated to overlap slightly at the edge of the spread width, and overlap will be considered to be negligible. The spreader is to be calibrated to deliver one-half of the recommended rate per pass. The material will be applied in two passes made at right angles to each other. A 75-ft test strip will be used for calibration. The material comes in 40-lb bags.

How much insecticide will be released on the test strip when the spreader is properly calibrated?

How many bags of material will be needed for the treatment?

SPRAYER CALIBRATION

In some ways, the principles of sprayer calibration are the same as those for spreader calibration. A test strip will be measured and the machine will be operated over a known area. The amount of material, in this case a liquid, released on the test area will be determined. However, there are also some important differences. The type and size of nozzles and the pressure generated by the pump are two variables that have a considerable impact on the application rate. Operating speed will also be a major factor, as it is in the application of dry materials, and a uniform speed is an absolute necessity for proper application.

There are many different types of sprayers. They vary greatly in their size, number of nozzles, spray pattern, and other features. No attempt will be made to deal with all types. Fortunately, the procedures for calibration are basically the same for all of the different types.

The first step in calibration is to read the instructions in the manual. Be sure that the sprayer is properly equipped with the right nozzles and that the boom height is properly set for the type of nozzle being used. Operate the sprayer with clean water to be sure that all nozzles are working properly. There are usually tables available that include calibration information at given pressures and operating speeds. These figures should always be checked by independent calibration procedures—as will be outlined in this chapter—to verify that the printed information is correct. Nozzle wear can have a considerable effect on application rate and nozzles should be checked on a regular basis and changed when wear becomes excessive.

The sprayers that will be used in the following examples are standard boom sprayers with nozzles on a metal bar mounted behind the unit (Figure 5.10).

Example 5.5

Determine the number of gallons per acre released by a boom sprayer with a 15 ft boom and 10 nozzles.

Step 1. The pressure of the pump and the speed of operation are two factors that affect application rate. Both of these factors will be under the control of the applicator. Begin by choosing a pressure and speed that are

Figure 5.10. Boom sprayer.

in a reasonable range for the nozzle type and the type of application that is to be made. Once these have been selected it is very important they be maintained throughout the application process.

For this example, a pressure of 30 psi (pounds per square inch) will be chosen and the equipment will be operated in first gear at 1,500 RPM (revolutions per minute). If no tachometer is available to measure RPMs, be sure to operate the equipment at a constant throttle setting.

Step 2. Speedometers are generally very inaccurate at low speeds. Begin the process by accurately determining the operating speed. In this case, a 100-ft test strip will be used. The sprayer is operated over the 100-ft test strip at the RPM setting and in the chosen gear. The time required to travel the 100-ft distance is measured with a stopwatch. This step should be completed 2 or 3 times and that average time should be calculated. In this test, the time required to cover the 100-ft strip is 14 sec.

Step 3. Determine the area covered by the sprayer when the test strip is covered.

100 ft

15 ft

When a 15-ft-wide boom is operated over a 100-ft test area, $100 \times 15 = 1{,}500 \text{ ft}^2$.

It has now been determined that this sprayer, at this operating speed, will cover $1{,}500 \text{ ft}^2$ in 14 sec.

Step 4. Measure the flow rate of each nozzle. This will be done while the sprayer is stationary, but be sure that the pressure of the pump (in this case 30 psi) is set at the same level as will be used for the application.

Collect the flow from each nozzle and determine the number of ounces released over a set period of time (Figure 5.11). If the nozzles vary significantly in their flow rate (more than 10%), nozzles may need to be changed. The amount of time can vary, but choosing the time required for the spray unit to cover the test strip (in this case 14 sec) will simplify the process.

In this example, the average flow per nozzle has been determined to be 17.5 oz in 14 sec.

Step 5. Calculate the number of gallons released on the test strip. In this case, there are 10 nozzles, each of which release 17.5 oz, for a total of $17.5 \times 10 = 175$ oz.

There are 128 oz/gal. Therefore

$$\frac{175}{128} = 1.37 \text{ gal}$$

A total of 1.37 gal of liquid would be released on the 1,500-ft test strip.

If 1.37 gal are released on $1{,}500 \text{ ft}^2$, how many gallons would be released on $43{,}560 \text{ ft}^2$ (1 ac)?

$$\frac{1.37 \text{ gal}}{1{,}500 \text{ ft}^2} = \frac{X \text{ gal}}{43{,}560 \text{ ft}^2}$$

$$1{,}500 \, X = (1.37)(43{,}560)$$

$$X = \frac{59{,}677}{1{,}500}$$

$$X = 39.8 \text{ gal}$$

Figure 5.11. Collecting flow from nozzles.

The application rate of this sprayer is 39.8, or approximately 40 gal/ac.

Step 6. Verify the application rate on a larger area. For instance, a 2.5-ac fairway would require $2.5 \times 40 = 100$ gal.

Problem 5.5

Determine the application rate in gallons per acre for a 12-ft-wide boom sprayer with 8 nozzles. The test strip is 100 ft long and the sprayer travels this distance in 12 sec. In an 18-sec flow rate test, each nozzle released an average of 30 oz.

Example 5.6

An 18-ft-wide boom sprayer with 12 nozzles is operated at 8 mph. In a flow rate test, each nozzle released an average of 124 oz/min. What is the application rate in gallons per acre for this sprayer?

Step 1. In this case the speed of operation in mph is known. This provides the information needed to calculate the application rate. Remember that mph means miles per hour. In 60 min (1 hr) this sprayer will travel 8 miles. One mile is 5,280 ft, and 8 miles is $8 \times 5,280 = 42,240$ ft. The sprayer is 18 ft wide, therefore in 60 min of operation, this sprayer will cover:

42,240 ft

18 ft

$$(18)(42,240) = 760,320 \text{ ft}^2$$

a total of 760,320 ft² in 60 min (1 hr).

Step 2. Each nozzle releases 124 oz/min. There are 12 nozzles, and the entire boom will release $124 \times 12 = 1,488$ oz/min. If 1,488 oz are released in 1 min, how many oz are released in 60 min?

$$(1,488)(60) = 89,280 \text{ oz}$$

A total of 89,280 oz would be released by this sprayer in 60 min (1 hr).

Step 3. If 89,280 oz are released when the sprayer is operated over a 760,320 ft² area, how much will be released when the sprayer is operated over 43,560 ft² (1 ac)?

$$\frac{89,280 \text{ oz}}{760,320 \text{ ft}^2} = \frac{X \text{ oz}}{43,560 \text{ ft}^2}$$

$$760,320 \text{ X} = (89,280)(43,560)$$

$$X = \frac{3,889,036,800}{760,320}$$

$$X = 5,115 \text{ oz}$$

There are 128 oz per gal, therefore:

$$\frac{5,115}{128} = 40 \text{ gal}$$

the application rate of this sprayer is 40 gal/ac.

Step 4. Again, this should be verified on a larger area measuring an acre or more.

Problem 5.6

A 15-ft-wide boom sprayer with 12 nozzles is to be operated at 6 mph. Each nozzle releases an average of 96 oz in 20 sec. What is the application rate in gal/ac for this sprayer?

Example 5.7

The sprayer in Example 5.6 was calculated to release 40 gal/ac. It has a 100-gal tank. A 4EC herbicide is to be applied to the 35 ac of fairways with this sprayer. The material will be applied at 1.5 lb a.i./ac.

How much herbicide is needed to treat the 35 ac?

How many oz of the herbicide will be placed in the 100-gal tank each time it is filled?

Step 1. If 1.5 lb a.i. is to be applied per acre, how many lb a.i. will be needed to treat 35 ac?

$$\frac{1.5 \text{ lb a.i.}}{1 \text{ ac}} = \frac{X \text{ lb a.i.}}{35 \text{ ac}}$$

$$X = (1.5)(35)$$

$$X = 52.5 \text{ lb a.i.}$$

If there are 4 lb a.i./gal, how many gallons will be needed to apply 52.5 lb a.i.?

$$\frac{1 \text{ gal}}{4 \text{ lb a.i.}} = \frac{X \text{ gal}}{52.5 \text{ lb a.i.}}$$

$$4 X = (1)(52.5)$$

$$X = \frac{52.5}{4}$$

$$X = 13.1 \text{ gal}$$

Slightly more than 13 gal (13.1) will be required to treat the 35 ac at 1.5 lb a.i./ac with the 4EC material.

Step 2. The sprayer will release 40 gal/ac. If there is to be 1.5 lb a.i. in every 40 gal of water, how many lb a.i. should be placed in the 100-gal tank?

$$\frac{1.5 \text{ lb a.i.}}{40 \text{ gal}} = \frac{X \text{ lb a.i.}}{100 \text{ gal}}$$

$$40 X = (1.5)(100)$$

$$X = \frac{150}{40}$$

$$X = 3.75 \text{ a.i.}$$

If 1 gal of the herbicide contains 4 lb a.i., how much of the herbicide should be placed in the tank to obtain 3.75 lb a.i.?

$$\frac{1 \text{ gal}}{4 \text{ lb a.i.}} = \frac{X \text{ gal}}{3.75 \text{ lb a.i.}}$$

$$4 X = (1)(3.75)$$

$$X = \frac{3.75}{4}$$

$$X = 0.94 \text{ gal}$$

If there are 128 oz/gal, how many oz will be placed in the tank?

$$\frac{128 \text{ oz}}{1 \text{ gal}} = \frac{X \text{ oz}}{0.94 \text{ gal}}$$

$$X = (128)(0.94)$$

$$X = 120.3 \text{ oz}$$

Place a few gallons of water in the tank. Add 120.3 oz (0.94 gal) of the herbicide and fill it to 100 gal with water. Every acre will receive 40 gal of liquid, which will contain the 1.5 lb a.i. of the herbicide.

Problem 5.7

A 12-ft-wide boom sprayer with 8 nozzles releases 26.5 oz/nozzle/min. It has been timed to cover a 100-ft test strip in 15 sec. The tank on the sprayer is 150 gal.

What is the application rate for this sprayer in gal/ac at this operating speed?

A 50WP insecticide is to be applied to 30 ac of greens at 1.25 lb a.i./ac. How much total material will be needed to make the treatment? How much material will be placed in the 150-gal tank when the sprayer is filled?

6

Irrigation Calculations

The subject of irrigation calculations is very complex, and most of the detailed mathematics involved in the design of an irrigation system are best left to an expert on the subject. However, there are many practical problems involving irrigation of turf that are the responsibility of the superintendent. These problems include total water use, the cost of irrigation water, and the capacity of storage lakes.

The best place to begin in working water problems on the golf course is with the concept of the acre foot (ac-ft). An acre foot is the amount of water that would be required to cover an acre ($43,560$ ft^2) to depth of 1 ft. The conversion factor used to determine the number of gallons in an acre-foot is as follows:

$$1 \text{ ac-ft} = 325,828.8 \text{ gal}$$

To cover 5 ac with 1 ft of water would require:

$$(5)(325,828.8) = 1,629,144 \text{ gal of water}$$

The next step requires some imagination. Visualize 1 ac covered by 1 ft of water. Then, visualize twelve 1-in. sections of water on that acre.

12 1- inch X 1- acre sections

109

These 12 inches equal one foot. The number of gallons required to cover 1 ac to a depth of 1 in. is one-twelfth of 1 ac-ft:

$$325,828.8 \text{ gal}/12 = 27,152.4 \text{ gal in 1 ac-in.}$$

Visualizing and understanding this will allow for the solving of a variety of problems.

Example 6.1

If 40 ac of turf were to be irrigated with 1 in. of water, how many gallons would need to be applied to the area?

There are 40 ac, each receiving 1 ac-in.. There are 27,152.4 gal of water in 1 ac-in. Therefore:

$$(27,152.4)(40) = 1,086,096 \text{ gal}$$

would be needed to apply 1 in. of water to 40 ac.

Problem 6.1

Eight acres of fairway are to be irrigated with 2 in. of water over the next two weeks. How much water will be needed to make this application?

Example 6.2

The management of an 18-hole golf course is considering the possibility of connecting to the city water system. There are 55 ac of irrigated fairways and 110,000 ft² of greens and tees.

The city manager has requested figures on how much water would have to be supplied to the course in a peak irrigation week in midsummer. The course management wants an estimate of the total water cost for the season, given a cost of $0.03 per cubic foot (ft³) of water.

To solve these problems, superintendents must make certain assumptions that will vary with the conditions found on each golf course. Good estimates of water use rates usually can be obtained from the local supplier of irrigation equipment. For this problem, it will be assumed that a total of 1.2 in. irrigation, including adjustments for evaporation, will be needed in a peak irrigation week on the fairways. A figure of 1.8 in./wk will be used for greens and tees.

Begin by Determining Total Water Use for a 1-Week Period

(A) Fairways: There are 55 ac of irrigated fairways that are to receive 1.2 in. of water during a peak week of irrigation. It has already been calculated that 1 in. of water on 1 ac will contain 27,152.4 gal:

1) $\dfrac{27,152.4}{1 \text{ in.}} = \dfrac{X \text{ gal}}{1.2 \text{ in.}}$

2) X = (27,152.4 gal)(1.2 in.)

3) X = 32,582.9 gal to apply 1.2 in. to 1 acre

4) (32,582.9 gal)(55 acres) = 1,792,059.5 gal of water will be required in 1 wk to apply 1.2 in. of water to 55 ac of fairways.

(B) Greens and tees: In this case, 1.8 in. of water will be needed on 110,000 ft².

1) $\dfrac{27,152.4}{1 \text{ in.}} = \dfrac{X \text{ gal}}{1.8 \text{ in.}}$

2) X = (27,152.4 gal)(1.8 in.)

3) X = 48,874.3 gal will be required to apply 1.8 in. of water to 1 ac. $(43,560 \text{ ft}^2)$

4) $\dfrac{48,874.3 \text{ gal}}{43,560 \text{ ft}^2} = \dfrac{X \text{ gal}}{110,000 \text{ ft}^2}$

5) (43,560)(X) = (48,874.3)(110,000)

6) X = 5,376,173,000/43,560

7) X = 123,420 gal of water will be required in 1 wk to apply 1.8 in. of water to 110,000 ft^2 of greens and tees.

(C) The total water requirement during a peak irrigation week:

$$\begin{array}{r} 1,792,059.5 \text{ gal} \\ + \ 123,420.0 \text{ gal} \\ \hline 1,915,479.5 \text{ gal} \end{array}$$ is the total water use for a 1-wk period.

Solving the problem of the cost of water during the season requires assumptions that will vary with soil type, course location, average rainfall, etc. For this situation, it will be assumed that 15 in. of irrigation water will be required for fairways and 21 in. will be required for greens and tees during the season.

Determine the Cost of Water for One Season

(A) Fairways: It has already been calculated that 1,792,059.5 gal of water will be needed to apply 1.2 in. of water to 55 ac of fairways. How much water will be needed to apply 15 in.?

1) $\dfrac{1,792,059.5 \text{ gal}}{1.2 \text{ in.}} = \dfrac{X \text{ gal}}{15 \text{ in.}}$

2) (1.2)(X) = (1,792,059.5)(15)

3) X = 26,880,892/1.2

4) X = 22,400,743 gal to irrigate the fairways for one season.

(B) Greens and Tees: It has also been calculated that 123,420 gal are needed to apply 1.8 in. of water to greens and tees. How much water will be needed to apply 21 in.?

1) $\dfrac{123,420 \text{ gal}}{1.8 \text{ in.}} = \dfrac{X \text{ gal}}{21 \text{ in.}}$

2) $(1.8)(X) = (123,420)(21)$

3) $X = 2,591,820/1.8$

4) $X = 1,439,900$ gal to irrigate the greens and tees for one season

(C) Total water required for the season to irrigate fairways, greens, and tees:

$$\begin{array}{r} 22,400,743 \text{ gal} \\ + 1,439,900 \text{ gal} \\ \hline 23,840,643 \text{ gal} \end{array}$$ is the total water use for one season.

(D) Costs: The cost of water is based on a charge of $0.03/ft^3. Determining the total cost will require one additional conversion factor: (1 ft^3 = 7.4805 gal)

1) $\dfrac{1 \text{ ft}^3}{7.4805 \text{ gal}} = \dfrac{X \text{ ft}^3}{23,840,643 \text{ gal}}$

2) $X = 23,840,643/7.4805$

3) $X = 3,187,038.7 \text{ ft}^3$

At $0.03/ft^3, the total cost of water is estimated to be:

4) $(3,187,038.7)(0.03) = \$95,611.16$

Problem 6.2

The department of natural resources is monitoring the amount of irrigation water used on your golf course. The golf course has 70 ac of fairways that receive 1.6 in. of water per week. There are 130,000 ft^2 of irrigated greens and tees, with a weekly water use rate of 1.9 in. Total irrigation for a normal season equals 19 in. for fairways and 29 in. for greens and tees. How many cubic feet of water does the golf course use in one season?

Example 6.3

Similar methods can be used to determine how much water is on hand in storage facilities.

In this example, the amount of water in a storage lake will be determined.

The lake has a surface area of 460,000 ft^2. Its average depth has been determined to be 8 ft. How many gallons of water are in the lake?

Begin by determining the number of ac-ft of water in the lake:

1) $\dfrac{1 \text{ ac}}{43,560 \text{ ft}^2} = \dfrac{X \text{ ac}}{460,000 \text{ ft}^2}$

2) $43,460 \ X = 460,000$

3) $X = \dfrac{460,000}{43,560}$

4) $X = 10.56$ ac of surface area

The average depth of the lake has been determined to be 8 ft. Therefore there are:

$$(10.56)(8) = 84.48 \text{ ac-ft}$$

in the lake.

There are 325,828.8 gal in 1 ac-ft.

1) $\dfrac{325,828.8 \text{ gal}}{1 \text{ ac - ft}} = \dfrac{X \text{ gal}}{84.48 \text{ ac - ft}}$

2) $X = 27,526,017$ gal

There are 27,526,017 gal in the storage lake.

Example 6.4

There are 75 ac of turf on the course that are to be irrigated from the storage lake in Example 6.3. How many inches of water could be applied to the 75 ac? Evaporation will not be considered in this problem. (In the "real world," figures on evaporation should be obtained for the region and included into the calculation.)

There are 27,152.4 gal in 1 ac-in. There are 75 ac to be irrigated. If 1 in. of water were applied to each acre,

$$(27,152.4 \text{ gal})(75) = 2,036,430 \text{ gal}$$

would be needed for the application.

There are 27,526,017 gal in the lake. Therefore:

$$\frac{27,526,017 \text{ gal}}{2,036,430 \text{ gal}} = 13.52 \text{ in.}$$

of water could be applied to the 75 ac.

Problem 6.3

A storage lake on the golf course measures 740,000 ft², and its average depth is 12 ft. There are 60 ac of turf on the course. Disregarding evaporation, how many inches of water could be applied to the 60 ac during the season?

7

Seeding Rate Calculations

The golf course superintendent is the largest consumer of grass seed in the turfgrass industry. This is due mostly to overseeding in the southern states, large numbers of acres established every year, and increased acres of fairways converted to bentgrass.

The calculation of seeding rates begins with the information on the seed label. Understanding what goes into the seed mixture will help you in selecting the right seed mixture. Seed containers are required by law to list on a label an analysis containing important information about the seed.

An example of a seed label is below:

Seed Mixture Analysis	
Fine Textured Grasses	**Germination %**
32.35% Adelphi Kentucky bluegrass	96%
33.70% Majestic Kentucky bluegrass	96%
31.85% Parade Kentucky bluegrass	94%
Other Ingredients	
0.05% Weed seed	Tested 5/97
2.05% Inert matter	25# Net wt
0.00% Other crop seed	
No Noxious Weeds	
	X,Y,Z Seed Company
	Anywhere, USA

The information on the label includes:

- name of seed producer or seller
- seed lot number
- seed variety
- percent purity of each variety as expressed by germination
- percent live seed of each variety as expressed by germination

- percent of any weed or other crop seed present
- percentage of non-seed material present expressed as inert matter
- list by variety of any noxious weeds present and their rate of occurrence
- date of last seed testing for germination

The number of seeds per pound varies with nearly every turfgrass species. The characteristics of turfgrass seeds are listed in the table below:

Seed Counts of Common Turfgrass Varieties	
Variety	Approximate # of seeds/lb
Bahia grass	166,000
Bentgrass:	
colonial	6,200,000
creeping	5,800,000
velvet	8,200,000
Bermuda grass	1,700,000
Bluegrass:	
Canada	2,250,000
Kentucky	1,700,000
rough	2,225,000
Centipede grass	400,000
Fescue:	
chewings	500,000
red	463,700
tall	230,000
Redtop	4,800,000
Ryegrass:	
annual	227,000
perennial	300,000

Determining the percentage of pure live seed (PLS) in a seed sample is one of the most useful seed calculations. The PLS is defined as the pure seed in the lot that can be expected to germinate under laboratory germination test conditions. It is calculated by multiplying the percentage of pure seed listed on the seed label by the percentage germination. A seed lot with 95% pure seed and 90% germination would have a PLS percentage of:

$$(0.95)(0.90) = 0.855$$

This seed lot contains 85.5% PLS. If the lot weighs 50 lb, the weight of PLS would be:

$$(50 \text{ lb})(0.855) = 42.75 \text{ lb PLS}$$

Example 7.1

A 50-lb seed lot has the following information listed on the label:

Baron Kentucky bluegrass	25.0%
Adelphi Kentucky bluegrass	25.2%
Victa Kentucky bluegrass	25.1%
Pennlawn red fescue	23.3%
Crop seed	0.5%
Weed seed	0.5%
Inert matter	0.5%
Germination of bluegrass	90.0%
Germination of fescue	85.0%

(A) How many lb of PLS are in the lot?

The first step is to determine the percentage of PLS. This will have to be done separately for the bluegrasses and the fescue because the germination differs for the two species.

The total pure seed for the bluegrasses is

$$25.0 + 25.2 + 25.1 = 75.3\% \text{ pure seed}$$

The percentage PLS is calculated as follows:

$$(0.753)(0.90) = 0.68$$

The number of lb of PLS for the bluegrasses is

$$(50 \text{ lb})(0.68) = 34 \text{ lb}$$

The same calculations are used for the fescue:

$$(0.232)(0.85) = 0.20$$

$$(50 \text{ lb})(0.20) = 10 \text{ lb}$$

The total lb PLS in the lot is:

$$34 \text{ lb} + 10 \text{ lb} = 44 \text{ lb PLS}$$

The cost per pound PLS is another useful piece of information in making budgeting and purchasing decisions.

Example 7.2

A 100-lb lot of Majestic Kentucky bluegrass contains 96% pure seed and lists a germination of 89%. The price of the lot is $355. What is the cost per lb of PLS?

$$(0.96)(0.89) = 0.85$$

$$(100 \text{ lb})(0.85) = 85 \text{ lb PLS}$$

As was done with the fertilizer problems, write down dollars per lb PLS to prevent errors.

$$\frac{\$}{\text{lb PLS}}$$

In this problem, there are 85 lb PLS that sell for $355. The cost per lb PLS is:

$$\$355 \div 85 \text{ lb PLS} = \$4.18 \text{ per lb PLS}$$

Problem 7.1

There are two seed lots available.

The first (lot A) contains 85% pure seed and has a germination of 80%. The cost of a 50-lb bag of this seed is $125.

The second (lot B) contains 92% pure seed and has a germination of 94%. The cost of a 50-lb bag is $145.

If cultivar, % weed seed, and other variables are similar for the two lots, which will be the best buy?

Appendix A
Conversion Factors

1) Weight Measures

1 ounce (oz) = 28.349527 g = 0.0625 lb
1 pound (lb) = 16 oz = 453.59243 g
1 ton (U.S.) = 2,000 lb = 907.18486 kg = 32,000 oz
1 milligram (mg) = 0.001 g
1 gram (g) = 1,000 mg = 0.035274 oz = 0.0022046 lb = 0.001 kg
1 kilogram (kg) = 1,000 g = 35.273957 oz = 2.20462 lb
1 ton (metric) = 2,204.6 lb = 1,000 kg

2) Square (or Surface) Measures

1 square inch (in.^{2}) = 6.451626 cm^2 = 0.0069444 ft^2
1 square foot (ft^2) = 144 in.^{2} = 0.111 yd^2 = 0.0929 m^2
1 square yard (yd^2) = 9 ft^2 = 1,296 in.^{2} = 0.83613 m^2
1 acre (ac) = 43,560 ft^2 = 4,840 yd^2 = 4,046.873 m^2 = 0.404687 ha = 0.0015625 mi^2
1 square mile = 640 ac = 1 section = 258.9998 ha = 3,097,600 yd^2 = 2,589,998 km^2
1 square millimeter (mm^2) = 0.01 cm^2 = 0.000001 m^2 = 0.00155 in.^{2}
1 square centimeter (cm^2) = 100 mm^2 = 0.155 in.^{2} = 0.001076 ft^2
1 square meter (m^2) = 10.76387 ft^2 = 1,550 in.^{2} = 1.195985 yd^2 = 1,000,000 mm^2 = 10,000 cm^2
1 hectare (ha) = 2.471 ac = 395.367 rod^2 = 10,000 m^2 = 0.01 km^2 = 0.0039 mi^2
1 square kilometer (km^2) = 0.3861 mi^2 = 247.1 ac = 100 ha = 1,000,000 m^2

3) Cubic Measures:

1 cubic inch (in.^{3}) = 16.3872 cm^3 = 0.000579 ft^3 = 0.00433 U.S. gal

1 cubic foot (ft^3) = 0.80356 bu = 1,728 in.^{3} = 0.037037 yd^3 = 0.028317 m^3
= 7.4805 U.S. gal = 6.229 imperial gal = 28.316 L = 29.922 qt (liquid)
= 25.714 qt (dry)

1 cubic foot (ft^3) of water = 62.43 lb (1 lb of water = 27.68 in.^{3} = 0.1198
U.S. gal = 0.01602 ft^3)

1 cubic foot (ft^3) of dry soil (approximate) = 90 lb (sandy), 80 lb (loamy),
75 lb (clay)

1 bushel (bu) dry soil (approximate) = 112 lb (sandy), 100 lb (loamy), 94
lb (clay)

1 cubic yard (yd^3) = 27 ft^3 = 46,656 in.^{3} = 764.559 L = 202 U.S. gal =
0.764559 m^3

1 cubic centimeter (cc) = 0.06102 in.^{3} = 1,000 mL^3 = 0.000001 m^3

1 cubic meter (m^3) = 1.30794 yd^3 = 35.3144 ft^3 = 28.3776 bu = 264.173
gal = 61,023 in.^{3} = 1,000,000 cm^3

4) Volumes (U.S.—Dry)

1 quart (qt) = 67.2 in.^{3} = 2 pt = 1.1012 L = 0.125 pk = 0.03125 bu =
0.038889 ft = 67.2 in.^{3}

1 peck (pk) = 0.25 bu = 2 gal = 8 qt = 16 pt = 32 c = 8.80958 L = 537.605
in.^{3}

1 bushel (bu) = 4 pk = 32 qt = 64 pt = 128 c = 1.2445 ft^3 = 35.2383 L =
2,150.42 in.^{3}

5) Volumes (U.S.—Liquid)

1 fluid ounce (fl oz) = 2 tablespoons = 0.125 c = 0.0625 pt = 0.03125 qt =
0.00781 gal = 29.573 mL = 1.80469 in. = 0.029573 L

1 cup (c) = 16 tablespoons = 8 fl oz = 0.5 pt = 236.6 cm^3

1 pint (pt) U.S. = 16 fl oz = 32 tablespoons = 2 c = 0.125 gal = 473.167 mL
= 28.875 in.^{3} = 0.473167 L = 0.0167 ft^3

1 quart (qt) = 2 pt = 4 c = 8 gills = 32 fl oz = 57.749 in.^{3} = 64 tablespoons
= 0.25 gal = 0.946333 L = 0.3342 ft^3

1 gallon (gal) = 4 qt = 8 pt = 16 c = 128 fl oz = 0.1337 ft^3 = 3,785.4 mL =
231 in.^{3} = 8.337 lb water = 3.782 kg

1 milliliter (mL) = 1 cm^3 = 0.1 centiliter = 0.01 deciliter = 0.001 L = 0.061 in.^{3} = 0.03815 fl oz

1 liter (L) = 2.1134 pt = 1.0567 liquid qt = 0.9081 dry qt = 0.264178 gal = 10 dL = 1,000 mL = 33.8147 fl oz = 61.03 in.^{3} = 0.035 ft^3 = 0.02838 bu = 0.001308 yd^3

6) Linear (or Distance Measures)

1 inch (in.) = 25.4 mm = 2.54 cm = 0.0254 m = 0.083333 ft = 0.027778 yd

1 foot (ft) = 12 in. = 0.3333 yd = 0.060606 rod = 30.48 cm = 0.3048 m

1 yard (yd) = 36 in. = 3 ft = 0.9144 m

1 mile (mi) statute = 5,280 ft = 1,760 yd = 1,609.35 m = 63,360 in.

1 millimeter (mm) = 0.1 cm = 0.01 dm = 0.001 m = 1,000 microns = 0.03937 in.

1 centimeter (cm) = 10 mm = 0.01 m = 0.3937 in. = 0.0328 ft = 0.01094 yd

1 decimeter (dm) = 10 cm = 0.1 m = 3.937 in.

1 meter (m) = 100 cm = 39.37 in. = 3.2808 ft = 1.09361 yd = 0.001 km

1 kilometer (km) = 1,000 m = 3,280.8 ft = 1093.6 yd = 0.62137 mi

7) Dilutions

1 part per million (ppm) = 1 milligram per liter or kilogram = 0.0001% = 0.013 ounce by weight in 100 gallons = 0.379 grams in 100 gallons = 1 pound in 500 tons

1 percent (%) = 10,000 parts per million = 10 grams per liter = 1.28 ounces by weight per gallon = 8.336 pounds per 100 gallons

8) Miscellaneous Weights and Measures

1 micrometer = 0.00039 in.

1 acre-inch of water = 27,152.4 gal = 624.23 gal per 1,000 ft

1 pound per cubic foot = 0.26 g per in.^{3}

1 gram per cubic inch = 3.78 lb per ft^3

9) Approximate Rates of Application Equivalents (U.S. Measures)

1 ounce per square foot = 2,722.5 lb per ac

1 ounce per square yard = 302.5 lb per ac

1 ounce per 100 square feet = 27.2 lb per ac

1 pound per 100 square feet = 435.6 lb per ac

1 pound per 1,000 square feet = 43.56 lb per ac

1 pound per acre = 1 oz per 2,733 ft^2 (0.37 oz/1,000 ft^2) = 4.5 g per gal = 0.0104 g per ft^2 = 1.12 kg per ha.

100 pounds per acre = 2.5 lb per 1,000 ft^2 = 1.04 g per ft^2

5 gallons per acre = 1 pt per 1,000 ft^2 = 0.43 mL per ft^2

100 gallons per acre = 2.5 gal per 1,000 ft^2 = 1 qt per 100 ft^2 = 935 L per ha

1 quart per 100 gallons (approximate) = 10 mL per gal

1 pound per gallon = 120 g per L

1 kilogram per hectare = 0.89 lb per ac

Appendix B

Answers to Problems

Problem 1.1

Section A—Green (circle)

$(3.14)(55^2 \text{ ft})$ = Surface Area

$(3.14)(3,025 \text{ ft}^2)$ = 9,498.5 ft^2 of green

Section B—Fairway (trapezoid)

$[(600 \text{ ft} + 400 \text{ ft}) \div 2](200 \text{ ft})$ = Surface Area

$(1000 \text{ ft} \div 2)(200 \text{ ft})$ = Surface Area

$(500 \text{ ft})(200 \text{ ft})$ = 100,000 ft^2

Section C—Fairway (rectangle)

$(550 \text{ ft})(200 \text{ ft})$ = Surface Area

                       = 110,000 ft^2

Section D—Fairway (triangle)

$[(200 \text{ ft})(125 \text{ ft})] \div 2$ = Surface Area

$(25,000 \text{ ft}^2) \div 2$ = 12,500 ft^2

Total for Fairway (B + C + D)

$100,000 + 110,000 + 12,500$ = 222,500 ft^2 of fairway

Section E—Tee (oval)

$[(125 \text{ ft})(60 \text{ ft})](0.8)$ = Surface Area

$(7,500 \text{ ft}^2)(0.8)$ = 6,000 ft^2 of tee

Problem 1.2

Step 1: Length line = 330 yd.

Step 2: Offset lines are set every 30 yd.

Step 3: Total of offset lines = 620 yd. There are 9 ft² in one yd².

$$(620 \text{ yd})(30 \text{ yd}) = 18,600 \text{ yd}^2$$
$$(18,600 \text{ yd}^2)(9 \text{ ft}^2/\text{yd}^2) = 167,400 \text{ ft}^2 \text{ of fairway}$$

Problem 1.3

Step 1: Length line = 60 yd, width line = 30 yd.

Step 2: Offset lines are spaced every 10 yd.

Step 3: Totals of length lines are:

E = 15 yd, F = 13 yd, G = 17 yd, H = 18 yd, I = 19 yd

Step 4: Subtracted values of offset lines and total are:

E	30 – 15	= 15 yd
F	30 – 13	= 17 yd
G	30 – 17	= 13 yd
H	30 – 18	= 12 yd
I	30 – 19	= 11 yd
Total		= 68 yd

Step 5: Multiply the total by the distance between offset lines.

$$(68 \text{ yd})(10 \text{ yd}) = 680 \text{ yd}^2$$
$$(680 \text{ yd}^2)(9 \text{ ft}^2/\text{yd}^2) = 6,120 \text{ ft}^2$$

Problem 1.4

Step 1A: 36 radius measurements totaled 2,250 ft for collar + green.
Step 2A: Divide the total of the measurements by 36.

2,250 ft ÷ 36 = 62.5 ft (average radius)

Step 3A: Determine the area of a circle using the average radius.

Area = $(3.14)(62.5 \text{ ft})^2$
Area = $(3.14)(3,906.25 \text{ ft}^2)$
Area = $12,265.6 \text{ ft}^2$ for collar + green.

Step 1B: 36 radius measurements totaled 2,025 ft for green only.
Step 2B: Divide the total of the measurements by 36.

2,025 ft ÷ 36 = 56.25 ft (average radius)

Step 3B: Determine the area of a circle using the average radius.

Area = 3.14 (56.25^2 ft)

Area = 3.14 3,164.1 ft^2

Area = 9,935.3 ft^2 for green only

Step 5: Determine the area of the collar by subtracting the green only value from the collar + green value.

12,265.6 ft^2 – 9,935.3 ft^2 = 2,330.3 ft^2 of collar

Problem 2.1

a) To topdress 9,200 ft^2 to 1/32 in. depth:

$$h = 1/32 \text{ in. depth} = 0.03125 \text{ in.}$$
$$h = 0.03125 \text{ in.} \div 12 \text{ in./ft} (0.03125 \div 12)$$
$$h = 0.0026 \text{ ft}$$
$$\text{Volume} = (9,200 \text{ ft}^2)(0.0026 \text{ ft})$$
$$= 23.92 \text{ ft}^3$$
$$= 23.92 \div 27 \text{ ft}^3/\text{yd}^3$$
$$= 0.89 \text{ yd}^3 \text{ to topdress the green}$$

b) To topdress 9,200 ft^2 to 3/8-in. depth:

$$h = 3/8 \text{ in. depth} = 0.375 \text{ in.}$$
$$h = 0.375 \text{ in.} \div 12 \text{ in./ft}$$
$$h = 0.03125 \text{ ft}$$
$$\text{Volume} = (9,200 \text{ ft}^2)(0.03125 \text{ ft})$$
$$= 287.5 \text{ ft}^3$$
$$= 287.5 \div 27 \text{ ft}^3/\text{yd}^3$$
$$= 10.65 \text{ yd}^3 \text{ to topdress the green}$$

c) Topdress to fill 3/4 in. diameter × 3.5-in.-deep core holes (36 holes/ft^2) on a 9,200-ft green:

Radius of one core hole = 0.375 in.

Volume of one core hole = [(3.14)(0.375 in.)^2](3.5 in.)

= [(3.14)(0.140625 in.^{2})](3.5 in.)

= (0.4416 in.^{2})(3.5 in.)

= 1.5 in.^{3} per hole

= (1.5 in.^{3})(36 holes/ft^2)

= 55.64 in.^{3}ft^2

= 55.64 in.^{3} ÷ 1,728 in.^{3}/ft^3

Volume to topdress 1 ft^2 = 0.032197 ft^3/ft^2
Volume to topdress green = (0.032197 ft^3/ft^2)(9,200 ft^2)
= 296.2 ft^3
= 296.2 ft^3 ÷ 27 ft^3/yd^3
= 10.97 yd^3 to fill all core holes on 9,200 ft^2 green

Problem 2.2

How many square feet of green can be topdressed to a 1/8-in. depth with sand that is stored in a rectangular storage bin that measures 15 ft by 20 ft? The average height of the sand is 6 ft.

a) Determine the surface area of the pile.

Surface area of topdress pile = (20 ft)(15 ft)
= 300 ft^2

b) Determine the volume of the pile.

Volume of cube = (300 ft^2)(6 ft)
= 1,800 ft^3

c) Convert the volume for ft^3 to yd^3.

= 1,800 ft^3 ÷ 27 ft^3/yd^3
= 66.7 yd^3

d) Determine how many cubic yards are needed to topdress 1 ft^2 to a 1/8-in. depth.

h = 1/8 in. depth = 1 ÷ 8 = 0.125 in.
= 0.125 in. ÷ 12 in./ft
= 0.0104 ft
Volume for 1 ft^2 = (0.0104 ft)(1 ft^2)
= 0.0104 ft^3/ft^2
= 0.0104 ft^3/ft^2 ÷ 27 ft^3/yd^3
= 0.00039 yd^3/ft^2

e) Determine how much surface area the pile will cover.

66.7 yd^3 ÷ 0.00039 yd^3/ft^2 = 171,025.6 ft^2 can be covered with the topdress material in the rectangular bin.

Problem 2.3

How much sand, peat, and soil needs to be ordered to mix a 7-2-1 topdress mix to topdress 126,000 ft² of greens to a depth of 3/8 in.?

$$h = 3/8 \text{ in. depth} = 0.375$$
$$h = 0.375 \text{ in.} \div 12 \text{ in./ft}$$
$$h = 0.03125 \text{ ft}$$
$$\text{Volume} = (126,000 \text{ ft}^2)(0.03125 \text{ ft})$$
$$= 3,937.5 \text{ ft}^3$$
$$= 3,937.5 \text{ ft}^3 \div 27 \text{ ft}^3/\text{yd}^3$$
$$= 145.8 \text{ yd}^3 \text{ to topdress } 126,000 \text{ ft}^2$$
$$\text{Sand Volume} = (145.8 \text{ yd}^3)(0.70)$$
$$= 102.1 \text{ yd}^3 \text{ of sand}$$
$$\text{Peat Volume} = (145.8 \text{ yd}^3)(0.20)$$
$$= 29.16 \text{ yd}^3 \text{ of peat}$$
$$\text{Soil Volume} = (145.8 \text{ yd}^3)(0.10)$$
$$= 14.58 \text{ yd}^3 \text{ of soil}$$

Problem 2.4

Determine the volume of water in the pond that has a surface area of 1 ac and an average depth of 75 ft.

$$\text{Surface Area} = 1 \text{ ac} = 43,560 \text{ ft}^2$$
$$\text{Volume} = (43,560 \text{ ft}^2)(75 \text{ ft})$$
$$= 3,267,000 \text{ ft}^3$$
$$= (3,267,000 \text{ ft}^3)(7.4805 \text{ gal per ft}^3)$$
$$= 24,438,793.5 \text{ gal of water in the pond}$$

Problem 3.1

How many lb of N, P, and K are there in a ton (2,000 lbs) of a 23-3-15 fertilizer?

$$(2,000)(0.23) = 460 \text{ lb N}$$
$$(2,000)(0.03) = 60 \text{ lb P}_2\text{O}_5$$
$$(60)(0.44) = 26.4 \text{ lb P}$$
$$(2,000)(0.15) = 300 \text{ lb K}_2\text{O}$$
$$(300)(0.83) = 249 \text{ lb K}$$

Problem 3.2

How many lb of N, P, and K are there in a partially filled bag of a 15-5-10 fertilizer that contains 38 lb of material?

$$
\begin{array}{ll}
(38)(0.15) & = 5.7 \text{ lb N} \\
(38)(0.05) & = 1.9 \text{ lb } P_2O_5 \\
(38)(0.10) & = 3.8 \text{ lb } K_2O \\
(1.9 \text{ lb } P_2O_5)(0.44) & = 0.84 \text{ lb P} \\
(3.8 \text{ lb } K_2O)(0.83) & = 3.2 \text{ lb K}
\end{array}
$$

Problem 3.3

How much 15-3-10 fertilizer would be needed to apply 1 lb N per 1,000 ft^2 to 170,000 ft^2 of greens?

$$
\begin{array}{ll}
(X)(0.15) & = 1 \text{ lb N} \\
X & = 1/0.15 \\
X & = 6.66 \text{ lb 15-3-10} \\
1000\ X & = (6.66)(170,000) \\
X & = 1,132,200/1000 \\
X & = 1132 \text{ lb of 15-3-10}
\end{array}
$$

Problem 3.4

How much 17-5-10 fertilizer would be needed to apply 0.75 lb of N per 1000 ft^2 to 40 acres of golf course fairways? (1 ac = 43,560 ft^2.)

$$
\begin{array}{ll}
(X)(0.17) & = 0.75 \text{ lb N} \\
X & = 0.75/0.17 \\
X & = 4.4 \text{ lb 17-5-10 per 1000 ft}^2 \\
(43,560)(40) & = 1,742,400 \text{ ft}^2 \\
1000\ X & = (4.4)(1,742,400) \\
X & = 7,666,560/1000 \\
X & = 7,666.6 \text{ lb of 17-5-10}
\end{array}
$$

Problem 3.5

A starter fertilizer (13-25-6) is to be applied to 18 newly seeded tees. A total of 2 lb P is to be applied per 1000 ft^2. The tees average 5,000 ft^2 each. How much 13-25-6 will be needed?

(18 tees)(5000)	= 90,000 ft^2
(X lbs P$_2$O$_5$)(0.44)	= 2 lb P
X	= 2/0.44
X	= 4.55 lb P$_2$O$_5$
(X)(0.25)	= 4.55
X	= 4.55/0.25
X	= 18.2 lb 13-25-6
1000 X	= (18.2)(90,000)
X	= 1,638,000/1000
X	= 1,638 lb 13-25-6

Problem 3.6

The recommendation is that 3 lb of K$_2$O per 1,000 ft^2 be applied to 50 ac of fairways. How much potassium sulfate (0-0-50) will be needed to make the application?

(50 ac)(43,560)	= 2,178,000 ft^2
(X)(0.50)	= 3
X	= 3/0.5
X	= 6 lb 0-0-50/1000 ft^2
1000 X	= (6)(2,178,000)
X	= 13,068,000/1000
X	= 13,068 lb 0-0-50

Problem 3.7

There are 160,000 ft² of greens on the course. A total of 4 lb N/1,000 ft² is to be applied during the season using a 20-2-10. The soil test indicates that 3 total lb of K should be applied/1,000 ft²/yr.

How much additional potassium sulfate (0-0-50) will be needed to achieve the 3-lb K level?

(X)(0.20)	= 4 lb N
X	= 4/0.20
X	= 20 lb 20-2-10
(20)(0.10)	= 2 lb K₂O
(2)(0.83)	= 1.66 lb K
3 lb K – 1.66 lb K	= 1.34 additional K
(X)(0.83)	= 1.34 lb K
X	= 1.61 lb K₂O
(X)(0.50)	= 1.61 lb K₂O
X	= 1.61/0.50
X	= 3.2 lb 0-0-50 per 1,000 ft²
1,000 X	= (3.2)(160,000)
X	= 512,000/1,000
X	= 512 lb 0-0-50

Problem 3.8

An 18-2-3 liquid fertilizer contains 1.8 lb N per gallon, 0.09 lb P, and 0.25 lb K.

a) How many gallons of this fertilizer will be needed to apply 1 lb N per 1,000 ft² to 60,000 ft² of tees?

1.8 X	= (1)(1)
X	= 1/1.8
X	= 0.56 gal per 1000 ft²
1,000 X	= (0.56)(60,000)
X	= 33,600/1,000
X	= 33.6 gal 18-2-3

b) How much P and K was applied per 1,000 ft^2?

$$\frac{0.90 \text{ lb P}}{1 \text{ gal}} = \frac{X}{0.56}$$

1 X	$= (0.09)(0.56)$
X	$= 0.0504/1$
X	$= 0.0504$ lb P

$$\frac{0.25 \text{ lb K}}{1 \text{ gal}} = \frac{X}{0.56}$$

1 X	$= (0.25)(0.56)$
X	$= 0.14/1$
X	$= 0.14$ lb K

Problem 3.9

A 200-gal sprayer is calibrated to release 3 gal total solution per 1000 ft^2. The goal is to apply 0.5 lb N/1,000 ft^2 to 25 ac of fairways using a 16-2-3 liquid fertilizer that contains 1.54 lb N/gal.

$$(25 \text{ ac})(43,560) = 1,089,000 \text{ ft}^2$$

a) How many gallons of 16-2-3 will be needed?

$$\frac{1 \text{ gal}}{1.54 \text{ lb N}} = \frac{X \text{ gal}}{0.5 \text{ lb N}}$$

1.54 X	$= 0.5$
X	$= 0.5/1.54$
X	$= 0.33$ gal per 1,000 ft^2
1,000 X	$= (0.33)(1,089,000)$
X	$= 359,370/1,000$
X	$= 359.4$ gal of 16-2-3

b) How much water and how much liquid fertilizer will be placed in each 200-gal tank?

3 X	$= (0.33)(200)$
X	$= 66/3$
X	$= 22$ gal fertilizer
$200 - 22$	$= 178$ gal water

Problem 3.10

What is the cost/lb of N, P, and K for a ton (2000 lb) of an 18-5-9 fertilizer that sells for $216/ton?

$$(2,000)(0.18) = 360 \text{ lb N}$$
$$(2,000)(0.05) = 100 \text{ lb P}_2\text{O}_5$$
$$(100)(0.44) \quad = 44 \text{ lb P}$$
$$(2,000)(0.09) = 180 \text{ lb K}_2\text{O}$$
$$(180)(0.83) \quad = 149.4 \text{ lb K}$$

$$\frac{\$216}{360 \text{ lb N}} = \$0.60 \text{ per lb N}$$

$$\frac{\$216}{44 \text{ lb P}} = \$4.90 \text{ per lb P}$$

$$\frac{\$216}{149.4 \text{ lb K}} = \$1.44 \text{ per lb K}$$

Problem 4.1

A 10G insecticide is to be applied at 2 lb a.i./ac to 120,000 ft^2 of greens. How much of the insecticide will be needed?

$$(X)(0.10) \quad = 2$$
$$X \qquad\quad = 2/0.10$$
$$X \qquad\quad = 20 \text{ lb product/ac}$$
$$43,560 \text{ X} = (20)(120,000)$$
$$X \qquad\quad = 2,400,000/43,560$$
$$X \qquad\quad = 55.1 \text{ lb product}$$

Problem 4.2

A 75WP herbicide is to be applied at a rate of 10 lb a.i./ac to 40 ac of fairways. How much of this material must be purchased for the application?

$$
\begin{aligned}
(X)(0.75) &= 10 \text{ lb a.i./ac} \\
X &= 10/0.75 \\
X &= 13.3 \text{ lb product} \\
13.3 \text{ lb/1 ac} &= X \text{ lb/40 ac} \\
X &= (13.3)(40) \\
&= 532 \text{ lb of product will be needed to treat 40 ac}
\end{aligned}
$$

Problem 4.3

A 50DF insecticide is to be applied at a rate of 1.8 lb a.i./ac. How much is needed to treat 5 tees that total 60,000 ft^2?

$$
\begin{aligned}
(X)(0.50) &= 1.8 \\
X &= 1.8/0.50 \\
X &= 3.6 \text{ lb/ac} \\
43,560 \, X &= (3.6)(60,000) \\
X &= 216,000/43,560 \\
X &= 4.95 \text{ lb of 50DF insecticide}
\end{aligned}
$$

Problem 4.4

A 90DF fungicide is to be applied at 6 lb product/ac.

a) How much would be needed to treat 35,000 ft^2 of turf?

$$
\begin{aligned}
43,560 \, X &= (6)(35,000) \\
X &= 210,000/43,560 \\
X &= 4.8 \text{ lb of 90DF fungicide}
\end{aligned}
$$

b) How much a.i. was applied/ac?

$$(6 \text{ lb})(0.90) = 5.4 \text{ lb a.i.}$$

c) How much total a.i. was applied to 35,000 ft^2?

$$(4.8 \text{ lb})(0.90) = 4.32 \text{ lb a.i./35,000 ft}^2$$

Problem 4.5

A 60WDG preemergence herbicide sells for $98.00 for a 10-lb bag. The same active ingredient in a 5G sells for $42.00 for a 50-lb bag. Which is the most expensive?

$$(10)(0.60) = 6 \text{ lb a.i.}$$

$$\frac{\$98.00}{6 \text{ lb a.i.}} = \$16.30 \text{ per lb a.i.}$$

$$(50)(0.05) = 2.5 \text{ lb a.i.}$$

$$\frac{\$42.00}{2.5 \text{ lb a.i.}} = \$16.80 \text{ per lb a.i.}$$

Problem 4.6

A 3L herbicide is to be applied at 2 lb a.i./ac. How many ounces will be needed to treat 25,000 ft^2 of tees? (1 gal contains 128 oz.)

$$3 \text{ X} = (1)(2)$$
$$\text{X} = 2/3$$
$$\text{X} = 0.67 \text{ gal/ac}$$
$$43,560 \text{ X} = (0.67)(25,000)$$
$$\text{X} = 16,750/43,560$$
$$\text{X} = 0.38 \text{ gal}/25,000 \text{ ft}^2$$
$$(0.38 \text{ gal})(128 \text{ oz/gal}) = 48.6 \text{ oz of material}$$

Problem 4.7

A 4F fungicide is to be applied at 12 lb a.i./ac.

a) How much material in fluid ounces will be needed to treat a 9,000-ft^2 green?

$$
\begin{aligned}
4 \text{ X} &= (1)(12) \\
\text{X} &= 12/4 \\
\text{X} &= 3 \text{ gal/ac} \\
43{,}560 \text{ X} &= (3)(9000) \\
\text{X} &= 27{,}000/43{,}560 \\
\text{X} &= 0.62 \text{ gal} \\
(0.62 \text{ gal})(128 \text{ oz/gal}) &= 79.4 \text{ oz}
\end{aligned}
$$

b) How much material was applied per ac?

$$(3 \text{ gal})(4 \text{ lb a.i./gal}) = 12 \text{ lb a.i. ac}$$

c) How much a.i. was applied to 9000 ft^2?

$$
\begin{aligned}
43{,}560 \text{ X} &= (12)(9000) \\
\text{X} &= 108{,}000/43{,}560 \\
\text{X} &= 2.5 \text{ lb a.i.}
\end{aligned}
$$

Problem 4.8

A fungicide is available in a 4.5F for $150.00/gal, a 50WDG for $123.00 for a 4-lb bag, and a 1.5G for $45.10 for a 35-lb bag. What is the cost per pound a.i. for each material?

$$\frac{\$150.0}{4.5 \text{ lb a.i.}} = \$33.33 \, / \text{ lb a.i.}$$

$$(4 \text{ lb})(0.50) = 2 \text{ lb a.i.}$$

$$\frac{\$123}{2 \text{ lb a.i.}} = \$61.50 \, / \text{ lb a.i.}$$

$$(35)(0.015) = 0.53 \text{ lb a.i.}$$

$$\frac{\$45.10}{0.53 \text{ lb a.i.}} = \$85.09 \, / \text{ lb a.i.}$$

Problem 5.1

A 54-in.-wide drop spreader is to be calibrated to apply 1 lb N/1,000 ft^2 using a 10-3-6 fertilizer in a single pass. A 25-ft test strip will be used for the calibration. A catch tray will be attached to the bottom of the spreader. How many ounces of 10-3-6 fertilizer will there be in the tray when the spreader is properly calibrated?

54 in./12	= 4.5 ft wide
(4.5 ft)(25 ft)	= 112.5 ft^2
(X)(0.10)	= 1
X	= 1/0.10
X	= 10 lb 10-3-6
1,000 X	= (10)(112.5)
X	= 1,125/1,000
X	= 1.125 lb on 25-ft strip
(1.125 lb)(16 oz/lb)	= 18 oz

The spreader will be used to treat 130,000 ft^2 of tees. How many 50-lb bags will be needed to make the application?

1,000 X	= (10)(130,000)
X	= 1,300,000/1,000
X	= 1,300 lb 10-3-6
1,300/50	= 26 bags

Problem 5.2

A 5G insecticide is to be applied to the greens at a rate of 3.0 lb a.i./ac. A 48-in.-wide spreader will be used for the treatment. A 50-ft test strip will be used and the material will be collected on a plastic sheet. The spreader will be calibrated at 1.5 lb a.i./ac and two passes will be used to make the 1.5-lb a.i./ac treatment. How much material will be released from this spreader on the test strip when the spreader is properly calibrated?

(X)(0.05)	= 1.5
X	= 1.5/0.05
X	= 30 lb product/ac
48 in./12	= 4 ft
(4 ft)(50 ft)	= 200 ft^2

43,560 X   = (30)(200)
X   = 6,000/43,5600
X   = 0.138 lb
(0.138 lb)(16 oz/lb) = 2.2 oz of 5G on the 50-ft strip

There are 150,000 ft² of greens to be treated. The insecticide comes in 42-lb bags. How many bags will have been used if the treatment is properly made?

43,560 X = (30)(150,000)
X   = 4,500,000/43,560
X   = 103.3 lb
103/42   = 2.5 bags at 1/2 rate, or 5 bags at full rate

Problem 5.3

A rotary spreader that is designed to overlap from wheel track to wheel track is to be used to apply an 18-5-9 fertilizer to 160,000 ft² of tees in one pass. The rate of application is 0.75 lb N/1,000 ft². A test strip of 100 ft is to be used and the effective spread width has been determined to be 15 ft.

0.75/2   = 0.375 lb per 1000 ft² will be applied
                                        per pass
(X)(0.18)   = 0.375
X   = 0.375/0.18
X   = 2.1 lb fert./1,000 ft²
(15 ft wide)(100 ft long) = 1,500 ft²
1000 X   = (2.1)(1,500)
X   = 3,150/1,000
X   = 3.15 lb on test strip

If the material is in 33.3-lb bags, how many bags will be needed to make the treatment?

(X)(0.18) = 0.75
X   = 0.75/0.18
X   = 4.2 lb per 1,000 ft²
1,000 X   = (4.2)(160,000)
X   = 672,000/1,000
X   = 672 lb
672/33.3   = 20 bags

Problem 5.4

A rotary spreader is to be calibrated to deliver a 2G insecticide at a rate of 4 lb a.i./ac to 140,000 ft^2 of tees. The effective spread width is 11 ft. It will be calibrated to overlap slightly at the edge of the spread width, and overlap will be considered to be negligible. The spreader is to be calibrated to deliver one-half of the recommended rate per pass. The material will be applied in two passes made at right angles to each other. A 75-ft test strip will be used for calibration. The material comes in 40-lb bags.

How much insecticide will be released on the test strip when the spreader is properly calibrated?

(11 ft)(75 ft)	= 825 ft^2
4/2	= 2 lb a.i./ac will be applied per pass
(X)(0.02)	= 2
X	= 2/0.02
X	= 100 lb material per acre
43,560 X	= (100)(825)
X	= 82,500/43,560
X	= 1.9 lb on the test strip

How many bags of material will be needed for the treatment?

43,560 X	= (100)(140,000)
X	= 14,000,000/43,560
X	= 321 lb
321/40	= 8 bags at 1/2 rate or 16 bags at full rate

Problem 5.5

Determine the application rate in gal/ac for a 12-ft-wide boom sprayer with 8 nozzles. The test strip is 100 ft long and the sprayer travels this distance in 12 sec. In an 18-sec flow rate test, each nozzle released an average of 30 oz.

(12)(100)	$= 1200 \text{ ft}^2$
(30 oz per nozzle)(8 nozzles)	$= 240$ oz in 18 sec
1,200 X	$= (12)(43,560)$
X	$= 522,720/1,200$
X	$= 435.6$ sec/ac
18 X	$= (240)(435.6)$
X	$= 104,544/18$
X	$= 5,808$ oz
5,808/128 oz/gal	$= 45.4$ gal/ac

Problem 5.6

A 15-ft-wide boom sprayer with 12 nozzles is to be operated at 6 mph. Each nozzle releases an average of 96 oz in 20 sec. What is the application rate in gallons per acre for this sprayer?

(6)(5,280)	$= 31,680$ ft
(31,680 ft)(15)	$= 475,200 \text{ ft}^2$
(96.2)(12)	$= 1152$ oz
20/60	$= 0.33$ min
475,200 X	$= (60)(43,560)$
X	$= 2,613,600/475,200$
X	$= 5.5$ min/ac
0.33 X	$= (1,152)(5.5)$
X	$= 6336/0.33$
X	$= 19,200$ oz
19,200/128 oz/gal	$= 150$ gal/ac

Problem 5.7

A 12-ft-wide boom sprayer with 8 nozzles releases 26.5 oz/nozzle/min. It has been timed to cover a 100-ft test strip in 15 sec. The tank on the sprayer is 150 gal.

What is the application rate for this sprayer in gal/ac at this operating speed?

(26.5 oz)(8)	= 212 oz
(12)(100)	= 1,200
1,200 X	= (15)(43,560)
X	= 653,400/1,200
X	= 544.5 sec/ac
60 X	= (212)(544.5)
X	= 115,434/60
X	= 1923.9 oz
1923.9/128 oz/gal	= 15 gal/ac

A 50WP insecticide is to be applied to 30 ac of greens at 1.25 lb a.i./ac. How much total material will be needed to make the treatment? How much material will be placed in the 150-gal tank when the sprayer is filled?

(X)(0.50)	= 1.25
X	= 1.25/0.50
X	= 2.5 lb
X	= (2.5)(30)
X	= 75 lb
15 X	= (2.5)(150)
X	= 375/15
X	= 25 lb in 150-gal tank

Problem 6.1

X = (27,152.4)(2)
X = 54,304.8 gal
(8 ac)(54,304.8 gal/ac) = 434,438.4 gal

Problem 6.2

$(27,152.4)(19) = 515,895.6$ gal
$(515,895.6)(70) = 36,112,692$ gal
$130,000/43,560 = 2.98$ ac of greens and tees
$(27,152.4)(29) = 787,419.6$ gal
$(787,419.6)(2.98) = 2,346,510.4$ gal
36,112,692
 2,346,510
38,459,202 gal total
$38,459,202/7.4805 = 5,141,261$ ft^3

Problem 6.3

$740,000/43,560 = 16.99$ ac
$(16.99)(12) = 204$ ac ft
$(325,828.8)(204) = 66,469,075$ gal
$(27,152.4)(60) = 1,629,144$ gal to apply 1 in. to 60 ac
$66,469,075/1,629,144 = 40.8$ in.

Problem 7.1

Determine the less costly seed lot:

a) Lot A: 85% pure seed, 80% germination rate.

  percentage PLS $= (0.85)(0.80)$
       $= 0.68$
       $= (0.68)\ (50\ \text{lb})$
       $= 34$ lb PLS
  Cost $= \$125/34$ lb
       $= \$3.68$ per lb PLS

b) Lot B: 92% pure seed, 94% germination

  percentage PLS $= (0.92)(0.94)$
       $= 0.86$
       $= (0.86)\ (50\ \text{lb})$
       $= 43$ lb PLS
  Cost $= \$145/43$ lb
       $= \$3.37$ per lb PLS

c) Lot B is the best buy.

Index

Active ingredient 65–67
Analysis of fertilizer nutrients 35
Area measurement 1–17
Average radius method 14–17

Boom sprayer 98–108

Circle, area of 3
Cone, volume of 21, 29
Conversion factors 125–128
Costs 54–56
    of fertilizer 35–56
    of irrigation 113–118
Cube 19
Cylinder, volume of 20

Drop spreaders 75–86
Dry pesticides 57, 58–64

Fertilizer 38–44
    calculations 35–56
    cost 54–56
Irregular shapes 22
Irrigation
    cost 113–118
Irrigation calculations 109–118

Liquid fertilizers 50–53
Liquid pesticides 57, 68–74
Liquids
    volume of 32–33

Offset method 7–9
    modified 10–13
Oval, area of 4

Pesticide calculations 57–74
Phosphate 45
Potassium 45
Pure live seed (PLS) 120–122

Ratio of fertilizer nutrients 35
Rectangle, area of 2
Rotary spreaders 87–97

Sand
    volume of 22–31
Seed counts 120
Seed mixture analysis 119
Seeding rate calculations 119–123
Sprayer calibration 75–108
Spreader calibration 75–108
Soil
    volume of 22–31

Topdressing
    volume of 22–31
Trapezoid, area of 2
Triangle, area of 3

Volume calculations 19–33